CAKES
GALORE

VALERIE BARRETT

Published by MQ Publications Limited

12 The Ivories, 6–8 Northampton Street

London N1 2HY

Tel: 44 (0)20 7359 2244

Fax: 44 (0)20 7359 1616

email: mail@mqpublications.com

North American office

49 West 24th Street

New York, NY 10010

Email: information@mqpublicationsus.com

Website: www.mqpublications.com

Copyright © MQ Publications Limited 2006

Photography: Marie Louise Avery

Home Economy: Valerie Barrett

Styling: Rachel Jukes

Page Layout: Philippa Jarvis

ISBN 10: 1-84601-122-1

ISBN 13: 978-1-84601-122-1

9 8 7 6 5 4 3 2 1

Printed and bound in China

This book contains the opinions and ideas of the author. It is intended to provide helpful and informative material on the subjects addressed in this book and is sold with the understanding that the author and publisher are not engaged in rendering any kind of personal professional services in this book. The author and publisher disclaim all responsibility for any liability, loss, or risk, personal or otherwise, which is incurred as a consequence, directly or indirectly, of the use and application of any of the contents of this book.

CONTENTS

INTRODUCTION

Few can resist the temptation of a slice of homemade cake, whether it's the simplest jam-filled sponge or an elaborate, layered, and fancily decorated creation. Important in many countries and cultures, cakes are often the centerpiece on special occasions.

★ AN ANCIENT CRAFT ★

The first cakes were made when primitive people discovered how to make flour. The earliest known examples, discovered by archaeologists in the remains of Neolithic villages, were made from crushed grains, moistened, sweetened with honey, and cooked on a hot stone. For centuries, baking remained a very haphazard affair because it was difficult to control heat. The Ancient Egyptians were the first to develop reliable cooking methods and ovens, and evidence of the cakes they made can be seen in their tomb paintings. The Romans were also skilled bakers and learned to leaven their cake mixtures with yeast.

The word "cake" is Anglo Saxon in origin and has been around for centuries, but its meaning has changed over time. In Medieval times, a cake was any item that could be shaped into a small round patty—we still refer to a "cake" of soap and "fishcakes", Later, the word was used for small unsweetened breads. Eventually cakes became distinct from savory items and were usually yeast-leavened combinations of flour, nuts, dried fruits, and honey that resembled what we now know as "coffee cakes".

During the Renaissance, Italian cooks, famed for their baking skills, were employed in households in England and France. They introduced the forerunner to the sponge cake—a thin crisp cake, lightened by eggs and sugar whisked to a thick frothy mixture. By the mid-18th century, yeast had been largely replaced as a leavening agent by this whisked-egg method. The mixture was poured into metal or wooden molds, which, though often very elaborate, were sometimes just plain tin hoops set on a baking sheet. It is from these hoops that our modern cake pans evolved.

Initially, cakes were served as in-between-meal snacks with sweet wine. Elaborate cakes would often be made for displaying at banquets, but were rarely eaten; the idea of serving cake as a dessert didn't occur until the mid-19th century when "Service à la Russe" became fashionable. In richer households, the meal was served by servants, and diners were brought individual dishes one course at a time. At last dessert had been invented.

Gradually, baking ingredients became more readily available due to mass production and better transportation, and modern leavening agents, such as baking soda and baking powder, completely changed cake-making. The Victorians developed ovens with more reliable temperature control and the Victoria sandwich cake became a familiar tea-time treat. A few decades later, baking became a vital skill for young women: a "good" housewife was judged on her ability to bake cakes as well as prepare meals and clean!

After World War II, pre-packaged cake mixes were introduced as "time-savers" in American grocery stores by companies such as Betty Crocker. At first, the powdered mixture didn't sell well and it was discovered that housewives felt guilty using a product that was simply mixed with water. When the recipe was changed so that it needed an egg as well, sales rocketed and packet cake mixes became available all over the world.

★ CAKE-MAKING TODAY ★

The massive range and easy availability of ingredients and equipment have simplified cake-making, and the popularity of home-baking has risen. Easy travel and communication has increased our knowledge of cakes from around the world so that today we are as likely to make a Turkish semolina and sesame cake as we are a date and walnut loaf. This book contains a wonderful selection of cakes, from all-time classics to more contemporary recipes, to suit every occasion, whether you are a novice or an experienced baker.

DIFFERENT WAYS OF
Making Cakes

There are five standard methods of cake-making: creaming, straight-mixing, whisking, rubbing-in, and melting.

★ CREAMING ★

This is probably the most traditional method of cake-making—pound cakes and quick breads are made by this method. The fat and sugar are beaten together until the mixture is light in color and fluffy in texture, indicating that a large amount of air has been incorporated. Further air is trapped when eggs are beaten in. Sifted flour is then gently folded into the mixture. During baking, the fat melts and the leavening agent reacts with the liquid in the eggs to produce carbon dioxide. This, together with the trapped air, makes the cake rise.

All ingredients, especially butter and eggs, must be at room temperature, or the cake will not rise properly. (Soften butter in the microwave on low power for 10–15 seconds if you've forgotten to take it out of the fridge.)

★ STRAIGHT-MIXING ★

All the dry ingredients are combined in one bowl and all the wet ingredients in another. They are then mixed together. The texture of cakes made this way will be more open and less fine than a traditional creamed cake, but this method is much quicker and easier. Because the ingredients are not added gradually, there will be insufficient air in the cake for a really good rise, so additional baking powder is used in combination with self-rising flour. Beat the ingredients together for two minutes only, if you are making it by hand, or one minute if you are using a hand-held electric mixer. It is particularly important, with this method, to bake the cake immediately after mixing it because the baking powder will already be activated.

★ WHISKING ★

Whisked sponges are the lightest of cakes and often contain no added fat and only a small amount of flour. The eggs and sugar are whisked together for at least 10 minutes, until the mixture has roughly tripled in volume, is very pale and the whisk leaves a "ribbon" trail on top of the mixture when lifted out of the bowl. Often the mixture is initially whisked over hot water to dissolve the sugar, then further whisked until it has cooled. A huge amount of air is incorporated at this stage and no further leavening agent is needed. Finally, sifted flour, and sometimes other dry ingredients, such as unsweetened cocoa powder or ground nuts, are folded in with a large metal spoon to ensure that as little as possible of the precious air is lost.

A classic whisked sponge is made without butter and stays fresh for only a day or two. It has a light, airy, even texture. A genoise, or Genoese sponge, which is made in the same way, usually has a slightly higher proportion of sugar. After folding in the flour, a little melted butter, margarine, or oil is trickled down the side of the bowl and gently stirred in. This makes a moister cake and improves the flavor and keeping quantities. A jelly roll can be made from either type of whisked sponge; the addition of a spoonful of warm water will prevent the sponge from cracking as it is rolled into shape.

★ RUBBING IN ★

This method is used for cakes that are typically made with half, or less than half, fat to flour and yields a fairly open texture. It is often used for light fruit cakes. The fat is cut into small pieces, then rubbed into the flour with the fingertips until the mixture resembles fine breadcrumbs, then the remaining ingredients are stirred in. The butter should be cold and firm, but not too hard, so take it out of the fridge about 10 minutes before you need it.

★ MELTING ★

Often used for moist cakes, such as gingerbread and fruit cake, the fat, sugar, syrup, and sometimes fruit are all gently heated in a saucepan over the stove until just melted. The mixture is usually cooled before the eggs and remaining dry ingredients are stirred in. Fat should be at room temperature and cut into small pieces so that it melts before other ingredients are over-heated.

EQUIPMENT

You don't need a vast amount of equipment to make a cake: measuring equipment, a bowl, wooden spoon, and cake pan are the only essentials, but there is a huge range of items that make baking a cake even easier.

★ MEASURING UTENSILS ★

The success of a cake depends on the ingredients being in the correct proportions, so a set of accurate measuring spoons and cups is vital

Dry measuring cups are designed so you can level them off with the back of a knife to get an accurate measurement. Take particular care

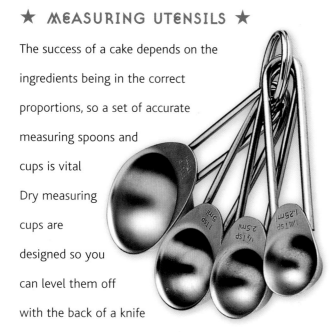

when measuring leavening agents: over-fill the spoon first, then level the top with the back of a knife.

★ BOWLS ★

Whether glass, ceramic, or stainless steel, a set of different-sized, heat-proof bowls for mixing, beating and melting ingredients is invaluable for cake-making. If possible, choose deep bowls for cake mixing rather than wide shallow ones.

★ SIFTER ★

Invest in at least two strong, fine stainless-steel or plastic sifters or mesh strainers; a larger one for sifting dry ingredients, such as flour, to remove any lumps and make it more aerated and easier to mix, and a small one for sifting icing sugar over the tops of baked cakes.

★ SPATULA ★

A flexible plastic or rubber spatula can be used to scrape the last little bit of cake mixture from the bowl and for smoothing the top of the cake level before baking. It is also useful for folding delicate ingredients, such as whisked egg whites, into cake mixtures.

★ WHISKS ★

Food processors and mixers are excellent for creaming butter and sugar together, whisking eggs and sugar to a thick foam and for beating egg whites. You should, however, always fold in dry ingredients by hand to avoid over-mixing the cake batter. Hand-held electric mixers can be used in the same way but are more convenient because they allow you to control the movement around the bowl. They can also be used in a bowl over a pan of near-boiling water when making whisked sponges. Wire balloon whisks and hand-held rotary whisks are good, but more time-consuming, alternatives.

★ PANS ★

These are available in all sorts of shapes and sizes, from round and square pans and rectangular loaf pans to petal-, heart-, and novelty-shaped ones. Look for tins

made from heavy-gauge metal; the thicker the gauge the less likely they are to warp or have hot spots. Aluminum is inexpensive, simple to clean, and responds well to changes in heat. It does however, dent easily, so treat it carefully, or, if you can afford it, choose anodized aluminum. Tin is also a good metal for bakeware, but it will rust unless thoroughly dried after use. Non-stick pans are excellent and make turning out cakes much easier; again, they need careful use and storage as they scratch easily. If you use pans with a dark non-stick lining, you may need to reduce the oven temperature slightly as dark colors absorb heat. Loose-bottomed pans simplify turning out cakes. You can also buy 'springform' cake pans, which open out, so that the sides of the pan can simply be lifted off the cake and base. They are invaluable for delicate cakes, which should not normally

be inverted after baking.

★ BAKING SHEETS ★

These can be used in combination with cake hoops and novelty cake pans without bases. They may be entirely flat or have a lip along the length of one side. Baking trays have a lip all around the edge. It is vital to choose good-quality, heavy ones, which won't distort at high temperature. For cake-making, avoid baking sheets that are very dark as they absorb more heat, which means that the base of the cake will burn more easily. (Dark sheets are intended for other kinds of cooking, such as baking bread.)

★ SUGAR THERMOMETER ★

This is the most reliable way to check the temperature of a boiling sugar syrup when making caramel or frostings such as crème au beurre.

★ TIMER ★

This is essential, particularly for light sponges and roulades, as even an extra couple of minutes in the oven can result in a dry, over-cooked cake. Most modern ovens have a timer, but a hand-held digital or rotating dial timer is useful, particularly if you want to go into another room while your cake is baking.

★ WIRE RACK ★

The best way to cool all cakes, whether they are turned out of their pans straight away or left to cool partially or completely in their pans, is to rest them on a wire rack. This allows air to circulate, so that the cake cools quickly and prevents trapped warmth, which would make the base soggy.

★ PIPING BAGS AND TIPS ★

These are useful for piping whipped cream, frostings, icing, and melted chocolate onto cakes to decorate them. Most piping bags are now made of nylon; the best are glued and double stitched along the seams to prevent splitting or leakage. You can also buy disposable plastic piping bags.

★ AIRTIGHT CONTAINERS ★

Because homemade cakes do not contain preservatives, they should be stored in an airtight container as soon as they are cool to keep them fresh. Cheesecakes and cakes covered with butter-based icing or cream topping, or containing ingredients such as fresh fruit, should be stored in the fridge.

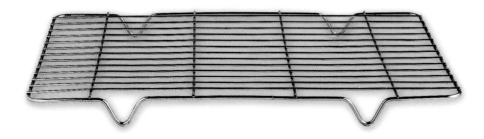

INGREDIENTS

Most cakes are made from just a few basics: flour, sugar, eggs, and usually butter, plus some flavoring ingredients, whether just a few drops of pure vanilla extract or a mixture of juicy fruits and nuts. Whatever your choice, always use good-quality, fresh ingredients to ensure that you make the best cakes.

★ FLOUR ★

Most cakes are made with soft wheat flour, either all-purpose or, more often, self-rising, which has added leavening agents. Because flour contains gluten, it is important not to beat the cake mixture too much after adding the flour, as doing so will develop the gluten, giving the cake a tough texture. Always check the "use-by" date on flour, as leavening agents deteriorate and your cake may not rise as well. Whole-wheat flour is milled from the whole wheat kernel. It is much coarser and heavier than white flour and gives cakes a denser, more filling texture.

★ LEAVENING AGENTS ★

Leavening agents are sometimes used in addition to self-rising flour, particularly in all-in-one mixtures where less air will be beaten into the cake mixture. Don't be tempted to add more than the recipe states or your cake will rise rapidly, then sink unevenly when removed from the oven, and the taste will be adversely affected. Baking powder is a mixture of cream of tartar and baking soda and releases carbon dioxide bubbles when it comes into contact with a liquid. Baking soda needs an acid ingredient as well as liquid to be activated. It is occasionally used in cakes that contain citrus juice, buttermilk, or yogurt.

★ EGGS ★

Eggs add richness to cakes and create volume. Size really matters: most of the recipes in this book use medium eggs, unless stated otherwise. Always use eggs at room temperature when making cakes, as cold eggs may curdle and cold egg whites produce less volume when whisked. Eggs will absorb flavors from other foods, so they should be kept in their box or in a separate compartment in the fridge and stored pointed end downwards, which helps to prevent moisture in the egg from evaporating.

★ BUTTER ★

Butter, either salted or unsalted, adds moistness, color, and flavor to a whole range of cakes. When using in creamed mixtures, it should always be soft, but not melting, so that it can be successfully combined with the sugar. Salted butter will keep well in the fridge for up to a month, unsalted for just two weeks, but both can be frozen for up to 6 months.

★ OTHER FATS ★

Stick margarine can be used as an alternative to butter in most recipes, and is less expensive, although it doesn't have the same creamy taste. Soft margarine is often used in straight-mix batters as it can be used straight from the fridge and blends quickly and easily. Avoid using low-fat margarines and spreads in cake-making as they have a high water content.

★ SUGAR ★

There are many different types of sugar used in cake-making, each with its own distinct characteristics. Granulated sugar has large granules and, in baking, is mostly used for sprinkling over cakes as a crunchy topping, as is demerara sugar, which has a deep golden color. Superfine sugar has fine grains and is most commonly used for cake-making as it creams beautifully with butter, trapping lots of air. Unrefined superfine

sugar has a pale gold color. Powdered sugar is a fine sugar, mostly used in cake icings and frostings as it mixes to perfect smoothness. Soft brown sugars are available in either light or dark brown and refer to any fine moist brown sugar made from a combination of refined sugar and a small amount of molasses. They will give a cake a rich flavor and a dark color. There are many other sweeteners used in cakes, including corn syrup, maple syrup, honey, molasses, and malt extract.

★ FRUIT AND NUTS ★

Both fresh and dried fruits are used in cakes, either folded into the mixture or for decorating the top. When fruit is dried, the flavor and sweetness is intensifed, so recipes containing a large amount of dried fruit often contain less sugar to compensate. Adding dried fruit does not affect the moisture of the mixture, so you can usually substitute one type of dried fruit for another in a recipe. Always use good-quality, plump moist dried fruit for the best flavor.

★ CHOCOLATE ★

Chocolate is a popular cake flavoring, and it is vital to use one with a high percentage of cocoa solids—70% or more is ideal. Unsweetened cocoa powder is a dark bitter powder than can be substituted for the same quantity of flour in many recipes. Avoid using drinking chocolate, unless specified by the recipe, as it contains only about 25% cocoa powder, the remainder being sugar.

★ ALCOHOL ★

Spirits, such as rum and brandy, sherry, and liqueurs are sometimes added to cake mixtures in small quantities to flavor them, and they can also be used to soak dried fruit before adding it to cakes. The alcohol will evaporate during baking, leaving a subtle taste behind. Some cakes are sprinkled with alcohol after baking, which gives a stronger flavor.

★ SPICES AND FLAVORINGS ★

Ground dried spices, most commonly cinnamon and ginger, feature in many cake recipes. Vanilla is also popular and is used in combination with many other flavorings, including chocolate. Citrus zest, especially orange and lemon, is another great flavoring for cakes; use unwaxed fruit if possible.

TROUBLESHOOTING

All the recipes in this book have foolproof, step-by-step instructions to help ensure your cakes are perfect every time. However, occasionally problems do occur, and it's important to find out what went wrong and why, so you can avoid the same mistake next time.

Q – *I don't have a pan in the right size. Is it okay to use one slightly bigger or smaller?*

A – For the best results, always use the pan size recommended in your chosen recipe as it may not bake successfully in a pan that is markedly different in size. It's not a good idea to use a smaller pan as the mixture may overflow. Sometimes you can use a slightly larger tin, but remember to adjust the cooking time if you do so, as the mixture will be shallower and will cook much faster. If you don't have a big selection of pans, it may be worth investing in a "multi-size" cake tin, which can be adjusted to the size you require. If you want to bake a round cake instead of a square one, or vice versa, a 7 inch round is the equivalent of a 6 inch square and a 9 inch round the equivalent of a 8 inch square.

Q – *I need a cake for a special occasion in a few months time. What sort of cake would be best to make in advance and how should I store it?*

A – Sponges made with the creaming method, such as a sponge cake, can be covered with fondant icing and will keep well for up to a week if wrapped in foil and kept in a clean airtight container. Alternatively, you can freeze an undecorated sponge for up to a month. If you want a cake that can be made well ahead, choose a rich fruit cake. This should be made two to three months before you decorate it to allow the cake to mature; its keeping qualities will improve further if you brush the top with alcohol, such as brandy or rum. After baking the cake, make sure it is completely cold, then wrap it in a double layer of greaseproof paper, then in foil.

Q – *I'm never quite sure when to take my cake out of the oven. How can I tell whether it's done or not?*

A – To test a baked sponge, press the center gently with a fingertip; it should feel spongy and give very slightly, then rise immediately, leaving no impression. A whisked sponge should be just shrinking away from the sides of the pan. To test a fruit cake, insert a fine skewer or toothpick into the center, leave it for 5 seconds, then remove. It should come away clean; if any mixture is sticking to it, bake the cake for a little longer.

Q – *Whenever I make a sponge cake and add the eggs to the creamed butter and sugar mixture, it curdles. Does this matter and how can I prevent it?*

A – If the creamed mixture curdles when you add the eggs, some of the air you've carefully beaten in will be lost and your cake won't rise quite as well. All the ingredients must be at room temperature before you start. If your kitchen is cold, stand the butter and sugar over a bowl of warm water for a few minutes, then place the bowl of beaten eggs over the water while you cream the butter and sugar. Add the beaten eggs a little at a time, beating thoroughly after each addition. If you see the mixture start to separate, beat in a spoonful of sifted flour before adding the rest of the eggs.

Q – *My sponge cakes always look perfect when I take them out of the oven, but they stick to the pan when I try to turn them out, no matter how well I grease them. What am I doing wrong?*

A – It's really disheartening when you damage your cake trying to remove it from the pan. For most cakes, you will need to line the pan with baking parchment—either just the base or the sides too—even if the pan is a non-stick one. If you use greaseproof paper, you may need to brush it lightly with oil or melted and cooled unsalted butter. Once removed from the oven, whisked sponges should be turned out straight away, but all other cakes benefit from being left in the pan for a few minutes to firm up and to allow the cake to shrink slightly from the sides. Some, such as rich fruit cakes, can be left in the pan until completely cool—each recipe will give advice on this. To remove the cake, run a palette knife around the edge of the pan. Turn out the cake onto a wire cooling rack covered with a clean dish towel, remove the lining paper, then cover the cake with another cooling rack. Invert both racks together and remove the top rack. Loose-bottomed cake pans make removal considerably easier, but don't use them for very wet mixtures or upside-down cakes, or some of the mixture may seep out during baking.

GRANDMA'S
FAVORITES

MISSISSIPPI MUD Cake

Top-quality chocolate will bring out the best in this rich and
tempting chocolate and nut extravaganza.

MAKES: 8–10 SLICES

1¼ cups/2¼ sticks butter, softened
1¼ cups superfine sugar
3 eggs, beaten
4 ounces dark bitter chocolate,
   melted
1 teaspoon vanilla extract
1½ cups all-purpose flour
4 tablespoons unsweetened cocoa
   powder
½ teaspoon baking powder
Pinch of salt
1 cup pecans, chopped

FOR THE FROSTING
⅔ cup/1¼ stick unsalted butter ½
   cup powdered sugar
5 ounces dark bitter chocolate,
   melted
Mini chocolate curls, for decorating

CAKE TIP
*Alternatively, try
using chopped walnuts
or a variety of chocolate
chips instead of the
pecans if preferred.*

1. Preheat the oven to 350°F. Grease a 9 x 5 x 3-inch loaf pan (or a 9 inch Bundt or ring pan).

2. For the cake, cream the butter and sugar together in a bowl until pale and fluffy, then gradually beat in the eggs. Add the melted chocolate and vanilla extract and mix well.

3. Sift the flour, cocoa powder, baking powder, and salt over the chocolate mixture and fold in with the chopped pecans. Spoon the mixture into the prepared pan and smooth the surface.

4. Bake in the oven for 40–45 minutes, or until a skewer inserted into the center comes out clean. Cool in the pan for 10 minutes, then turn out onto a wire rack and leave to cool completely.

5. To make the frosting, beat the butter in a bowl until pale and fluffy. Beat in the powdered sugar, then stir in the melted chocolate, mixing well. Place the cake on a serving plate, flat-base up, and spread with the chocolate frosting. Sprinkle mini chocolate curls along the center and serve in slices.

LAVENDER MADEIRA Cake

This is a buttery cake with a lovely, scented, summer flavor. Make sure the lavender is fresh and unsprayed.

MAKES: 8–10 SLICES

3 sprigs of fresh lavender, each about 4 inches long
3/4 cup/1 1/2 sticks unsalted butter, softened
3/4 cup superfine sugar
Finely grated zest of 1 lemon
3 eggs, beaten
1 3/4 cups self-rising flour

FOR THE FROSTING
4 tablespoons milk
3 sprigs of fresh lavender, each about 4 inches long
1 1/2 cups powdered sugar, sifted
Lavender food coloring (optional)
Extra small sprigs of fresh lavender, for decoration

1. Preheat the oven to 350°F. Grease and line a deep 8-inch round cake pan.

2. For the cake, remove the lavender flowers from the stalks; discard the stalks. Beat the butter and sugar together in a bowl until pale and fluffy. Add the lavender flowers, lemon zest, eggs, and flour and beat until smooth, well mixed and creamy.

3. Turn the mixture into the prepared pan and smooth the surface. Bake in the oven for 30 minutes, then reduce the oven temperature to 325°F and bake for another 15–25 minutes, or until a skewer inserted into the center comes out clean. Cool in the pan for 5 minutes, then turn out onto a wire rack and leave to cool completely.

4. To make the icing, put the milk and lavender sprigs in a very small saucepan. Bring just to the boil, then remove the pan from the heat. Cover and leave to stand for about 20 minutes. Strain the infused milk into a bowl and leave until cold.

5. Put the powdered sugar in a bowl and mix in just enough flavored milk (1–2 tablespoons) to make a thick coating consistency. Add a few drops of food coloring, if you like. Spread the frosting evenly over the cake and decorate with small sprigs of fresh lavender. Serve in slices.

RHUBARB & GINGER Cake

Banish the blues with this warming and delicious cake. The cornmeal adds an interesting texture and color to this cake, but ground almonds could be used instead.

MAKES: 8–10 SLICES

1¾ cups all-purpose flour
2 teaspoons baking powder
¼ teaspoon salt
⅔ cup cornmeal or instant polenta
2 eggs
3 tablespoons milk
1 teaspoon vanilla extract
½ cup/1 stick unsalted butter or
   margarine, softened
½ cup superfine sugar
1 pound fresh rhubarb, trimmed and
   cut into chunks
3 tablespoons sliced (drained)
   candied ginger

FOR THE TOPPING
½ cup all-purpose flour
¼ cup ground hazelnuts
5 tablespoons light brown sugar
½ teaspoon ground ginger
¼ cup unsalted butter, diced
Sifted powdered sugar, for dusting
Vanilla ice cream, crème fraîche or
   custard, to serve

1. Preheat the oven to 325°F. Grease and line a 9-inch springform pan fitted with a flat base.

2. For the cake, sift the flour, baking powder, and salt into a bowl. Stir in the cornmeal or polenta. Whisk the eggs in a separate bowl until thick, pale, and creamy and stir in the milk and vanilla extract.

3. In another bowl, cream the butter or margarine and sugar together until pale and fluffy. Fold in the dry ingredients alternately with the whisked egg mixture to make a thick batter.

4. Spoon the mixture into the prepared pan and smooth the surface. Arrange the rhubarb and candied ginger on top.

5. To make the topping, mix the flour, ground hazelnuts, brown sugar, and ginger in a bowl. Rub in the butter until the mixture resembles coarse crumbs. Sprinkle the topping mixture evenly over the rhubarb and candied ginger so that some pieces of rhubarb are quite thickly coated, while others are just dusted with the mixture.

6. Bake in the oven for 1–1¼ hours, or until the cake is firm to the touch and the crumb topping is golden brown. Test to ensure the rhubarb is tender by gently inserting a skewer into one of the exposed pieces.

7. Cool in the pan for 5 minutes, then remove the sides of the pan and transfer the cake to a serving plate. Dust with sifted powdered sugar and serve warm in slices with ice cream, crème fraîche, or custard.

RUM Cake

This cake makes an impressive dessert. Serve it warm with pan-fried bananas and vanilla ice cream for a sensational finish to a meal.

MAKES: 10–12 SLICES

Scant 1 cup/1¾ sticks unsalted butter, softened
1¼ cups light brown sugar
2 eggs, beaten
1⅔ cups all-purpose flour
½ teaspoon baking powder
1 teaspoon ground allspice
Pinch of salt
3 tablespoons dark rum
FOR THE TOPPING
¼ cup superfine sugar
3 tablespoons rum
3 tablespoons unsalted butter

CAKE TIP
This cake will freeze well. Simply cut into slices and wrap individually —that way you can take them out as and when needed. Perfect for lunchboxes and picnics.

1. Preheat the oven to 350°F. Grease and line a 10-inch loaf pan.

2. For the cake, beat the butter in a bowl until pale and creamy, then add the sugar and beat for a further 3–4 minutes.

3. Gradually add the eggs, beating well after each addition. Sift the flour, baking powder, allspice, and salt over the creamed mixture and fold in together with the rum.

4. Spoon the mixture into the prepared pan and smooth the surface. Bake in the oven for 50–55 minutes, or until the cake is firm to the touch and a skewer inserted into the center comes out clean.

5. Meanwhile, make the topping. Place the sugar, rum, butter and 2 tablespoons of water in a saucepan and heat gently, stirring until the sugar has dissolved.

6. Remove the cake from the oven. Using a toothpick, prick the top of the cake lightly, then pour over the rum syrup. Cool in the pan for 10–15 minutes, then turn out and serve warm or cold in slices.

PASSION Cake

A thick, indulgent layer of sweet, cream cheese frosting makes this cake extra special. Walnuts can be substituted for the pecans, if you prefer.

MAKES: 8 SQUARES

²/₃ cup safflower or sunflower oil

¾ cup packed light brown sugar

3 eggs, beaten

½ teaspoon ground cinnamon

½ teaspoon freshly grated nutmeg

5 ounces carrots, coarsely grated

1 banana, peeled and mashed

⅓ cup pecans, chopped

1²/₃ cup all-purpose flour, sifted

1 tablespoon baking powder

FOR THE FROSTING

²/₃ cup cream cheese or full-fat
    soft cheese, softened

Scant 1 cup powdered sugar, sifted

Finely grated zest of ½ orange

⅓ cup pecans, chopped (optional)

1. Preheat the oven to 350°F. Grease and line a deep 8-inch square cake pan.

2. Put all the cake ingredients into a large mixing bowl and beat together until well mixed.

3. Spoon the mixture into the prepared pan and smooth the surface. Bake in the oven for 45–50 minutes, or until golden and a skewer inserted into the center comes out clean.

4. Cool in the pan for 10 minutes, then turn out onto a wire rack and leave to cool completely.

5. Make the frosting. Beat the cream cheese, powdered sugar and orange zest together in a bowl until pale and fluffy. Spread the frosting over the top of the cake and sprinkle with pecans before serving, if you like. Cut into squares to serve.

BURNT-SUGAR Cake

MAKES: 8–10 SLICES

2¼ cups superfine sugar

½ cup boiling water

¾ cup/1½ sticks unsalted butter, softened

3 eggs, beaten

2¼ cups self-rising flour

1 teaspoon baking soda

¾ cup sour cream

FOR THE FROSTING & DECORATION

1 stick unsalted butter, softened

2 cups powdered sugar, sifted

3 tablespoons superfine sugar

CAKE TIP

When making the caramel syrup, use a long-handled spoon to add the boiling water to the melted sugar—and be very careful as the liquid will bubble fiercely.

1. To make the caramel syrup, cook 1 cup of the sugar over medium heat in a medium, heavy-bottomed saucepan, stirring occasionally until the sugar has melted. Cook, without stirring, until dark golden. Remove from the heat and carefully and gradually add the boiling water. Return the pan to the heat and simmer, stirring, for about 1 minute until the caramel has dissolved. Pour the caramel into a heat-proof measuring cup and set aside.

2. Preheat the oven to 350°F. Grease and line two 8-inch round cake pans.

3. Cream the butter and remaining sugar together in a bowl until pale and fluffy, then gradually beat in the eggs. In a separate bowl, sift together the flour and baking soda. In another bowl, mix together the sour cream and ½ cup of the cooled caramel syrup.

4. Fold the flour and caramel mixtures into the creamed mixture until well combined. Divide the mixture evenly between the prepared pans and level the surface. Bake in the oven for about 30 minutes, or until risen, golden brown and firm to the touch. Turn out onto a wire rack and leave to cool.

5. To make the frosting, beat the butter in a bowl until creamy, then gradually stir in the powdered sugar until combined. Add the remaining caramel syrup, mixing well. Sandwich the two cakes together with some frosting, then spread the remaining frosting over the top of the cake.

6. To make the decoration, lightly oil a baking sheet. Put the superfine sugar into a small non-stick frying pan and heat gently until the mixture turns a golden color, then pour it onto the prepared baking sheet. Leave until cold, then break the caramel into pieces and use to decorate the cake.

BUTTERMILK Cake

A light-tasting, simple cake that's incredibly easy to make and delicious to eat.

MAKES: 18 SLICES

¾ cup/1½ sticks unsalted butter, softened

1½ cups superfine sugar

1¼ cups buttermilk

1 teaspoon vanilla extract

Scant 2 cups self-rising flour

1 teaspoon baking powder

½ teaspoon baking soda

Pinch of salt

4 egg whites

CAKE TIP

If you can't get hold of buttermilk, use up ⅔ cup of milk mixed with ⅔ cup of plain yogurt.

1. Preheat the oven to 350°F. Grease and line an 11 x 7 x 2-inch cake pan or baking pan.

2. Cream the butter and sugar together in a bowl with 1 tablespoon of the buttermilk and the vanilla extract.

3. Sift the flour, baking powder, baking soda and salt together three times into a separate bowl. Stir the flour mixture and remaining buttermilk alternately into the creamed mixture, until well combined.

4. In a separate bowl, whisk the egg whites until stiff. Add one-third of the whisked egg whites to the sponge mixture to lighten it, then gently fold in the rest.

5. Pour the mixture evenly into the prepared pan. Bake in the oven for 35–40 minutes, or until just firm to the touch. Cool in the pan for 5 minutes, then turn out onto a wire rack and leave to cool completely. Serve in slices.

DARK JAMAICAN GINGER Cake

Ginger has been grown in Jamaica since 1547. This cake uses freshly grated ginger root in place of ground ginger, resulting in a deliciously moist cake with a wonderful mellow aroma.

MAKES: 10–12 SLICES

2 cups all-purpose flour
2 teaspoons baking powder
½ teaspoon baking soda
1 teaspoon ground allspice
½ teaspoon freshly grated nutmeg
1 cup/2 sticks unsalted butter
½ cup light brown sugar
2 tablespoons grated peeled fresh
   ginger root
½ cup evaporated milk
½ cup molasses
2 eggs, beaten

1. Preheat the oven to 350°F. Grease and line a 9-inch loaf pan.

2. Sift the flour, baking powder, baking soda, allspice, and nutmeg into a bowl. Add the butter and rub in until the mixture resembles breadcrumbs. Stir in the sugar and grated ginger root. Set aside.

3. Put the evaporated milk and molasses in a saucepan and heat gently until just warm, stirring. Pour this mixture into the flour mixture, add the eggs, and stir together until well mixed.

4. Pour the mixture evenly into the prepared pan. Bake in the oven for about 50 minutes, or until a skewer inserted into the center comes out clean. Leave to cool slightly in the pan, then turn out onto a wire rack and leave to cool completely. Serve in slices.

DEVONSHIRE HONEY Cake

This cake has a deep honey flavor complemented by the addition of orange zest. It is ideal for lunchboxes and picnics.

MAKES: 12–16 SLICES

1 cup unsalted butter
¾ cup clear honey
½ cup brown sugar
3 eggs, beaten
Finely grated zest of 1 orange
Generous 2 cups self-rising flour
½ cup pine nuts

CAKE TIP
For a change try using lemon zest instead of the orange and use slivered almonds in place of the pine nuts.

1. Preheat the oven to 325°F. Grease and line a deep 8-inch round cake pan.

2. Put the butter, honey, and sugar in a saucepan and heat gently, stirring, until the butter has melted. Increase the heat and bring to the boil, then boil for 1 minute. Remove the pan from the heat and set aside to cool.

3. Beat the eggs and orange zest into the honey mixture. Sift the flour into a bowl and gradually beat in the honey mixture until smooth and well mixed. Pour the mixture evenly into the prepared pan and sprinkle the top with the pine nuts.

4. Bake in the oven for about 50–60 minutes, or until firm to the touch. Cool in the pan for 5–10 minutes, then turn out onto a wire rack and leave to cool completely. Serve in slices.

LADY BALTIMORE
Sponge Cake

MAKES: 12 SLICES

1¼ cups/2¼ sticks unsalted butter, softened
1¼ cups superfine sugar
1 teaspoon vanilla extract
2 cups all-purpose flour
1 tablespoon baking powder
¼ teaspoon salt
1 cup milk
6 egg whites

FOR THE ICING
2 cups superfine sugar
2 tablespoons light corn syrup
4 egg whites
Pinch of cream of tartar
½ cup raisins
½ cup pecans, chopped
½ cup candied cherries, chopped
1 teaspoon vanilla extract

1. Preheat the oven to 350°F. Grease and flour two 9-inch round cake pans.

2. For the cake, cream the butter, 1 cup of the sugar, and the vanilla extract together in a bowl until pale and fluffy. Sift the flour, baking powder, and salt into a separate bowl. Fold the flour mixture and milk alternately into the creamed mixture.

3. In a separate bowl, whisk the egg whites until soft peaks form, then add the remaining ¼ cup sugar and whisk until the mixture is stiff and glossy. Add one-third of the whisked egg whites to the cake mixture to lighten it, then gently fold in the rest. Pour the mixture into the prepared pans, dividing evenly.

4. Bake in the oven for 25–30 minutes, or until the cakes are golden brown and just firm to the touch. Turn out onto a wire rack and leave to cool.

5. Make the icing. Put the sugar in a medium, heavy-bottomed saucepan with the corn syrup and 6 tablespoons of water. Stir to dissolve the sugar over a medium heat. Cook the sugar to medium ball stage, 245°F, without stirring. Meanwhile, whisk the egg whites and cream of tartar together in a bowl. When the sugar syrup has reached the correct temperature, pour it steadily into the egg whites, whisking continuously. Continue to whisk for 5 minutes, or until the icing is thick and creamy.

6. Stir the fruit, nuts, and vanilla extract into the cooled icing and use to sandwich the cakes together. Spread over the top and sides and serve in slices.

ITALIAN RICOTTA
Cheesecake

Ricotta cheese makes a delicious light cheesecake. This is ideal
served with fresh fruit for a tempting dessert.

MAKES: 10–12 SLICES

1½ pounds ricotta cheese
8 ounces mascarpone cheese
¾ cup superfine sugar
2 tablespoons cornstarch
4 eggs, beaten
2 teaspoons vanilla extract
¼ teaspoon ground cinnamon
2 teaspoons finely grated lemon zest
Pinch of salt

1. Preheat the oven to 300°F. Grease a 9-inch springform pan fitted with a flat base.

2. Beat the ricotta and mascarpone cheeses together in a large bowl until smooth, then stir in the sugar and cornstarch, mixing well.

3. Gradually add the eggs, beating well to combine. Stir in the vanilla extract, cinnamon, lemon zest, and salt, then pour the mixture evenly into the prepared pan. Bake in the oven for 50–60 minutes, or until the cheesecake is just firm to the touch.

4. Remove the cheesecake from the oven and leave to cool in the pan to room temperature, then cover with foil and refrigerate until ready to serve. Remove the cheesecake from the pan, place on a serving plate, and serve in slices.

CHOCOLATE MARBLE Cake

This is an impressive cake to serve to friends or family. You can also cover the cake with chocolate frosting if you like (see page 22 for Mississippi Mud Cake frosting).

MAKES: 6–8 SLICES

1 cup self-rising flour
2 teaspoons baking powder
Pinch of salt
Scant 3 tablespoons unsalted butter, softened
1 cup superfine sugar
2 eggs, beaten
$\frac{1}{2}$ cup milk
1 teaspoon vanilla extract
3 ounce dark bitter chocolate, melted
1$\frac{1}{2}$ cups powdered sugar
4 tablespoons unsweetened cocoa powder

1. Preheat the oven to 350°F. Grease and base line an 8-inch Angel cake pan.

2. Sift the flour, baking powder and salt into a bowl and set aside. Cream the butter and superfine sugar together in a separate bowl, then gradually add the beaten eggs, a little at a time. Fold the flour and milk alternately into the creamed mixture, then stir in the vanilla extract.

3. Pour half the mixture into a separate bowl and stir in the melted chocolate. Spoon the batters alternately into the prepared pan, then draw a knife through the mixture to create a swirled marble effect.

4. Bake in the oven for 35–40 minutes, or until the cake is firm to the touch and a skewer inserted into the center comes out clean. Cool the cake in the pan for 5 minutes, then turn out onto a wire rack and leave to cool completely.

5. Sift the powdered sugar and cocoa powder into a bowl, then stir in enough warm water, mixing to form a thick pouring consistency. Spread or drizzle the icing evenly over the cake. Serve in slices.

APPLE CRUMB Cake

A great balance of flavors and textures creates this fantastic cake, which is ideal for sharing with friends.

MAKES: 6–8 SLICES

²⁄₃ cup/1¼ sticks unsalted butter
1 pound cooking apples, peeled, cored, and chopped
½ teaspoon freshly grated nutmeg
1 teaspoon ground cinnamon
1½ cups all-purpose flour
¾ cup superfine sugar
2 eggs, beaten
3 tablespoons sour cream
1 teaspoon vanilla extract
½ teaspoon baking powder
¼ teaspoon baking soda
Pinch of salt

CAKE TIP
Serve this cake as a pudding with vanilla ice cream or a creamy custard.

1. Preheat the oven to 350°F. Grease and line a deep 8-inch round cake pan.

2. Melt 2 tablespoons of the butter in a small saucepan. Add the apples, sprinkle in the nutmeg and half the cinnamon, and stir to coat the apples in the butter. Place a disk of non-stick baking paper on top of the apples, reduce the heat, and cook gently, stirring occasionally, for 5–10 minutes, or until the apples are tender. Remove the pan from the heat.

3. In a bowl, lightly rub 2 tablespoons of the flour, 2 tablespoons of the remaining butter, and 2 tablespoons of the sugar together, until the mixture forms large clumps. Set this crumb topping aside.

4. In a separate bowl, cream the remaining butter and sugar together, then gradually beat in the eggs. Beat in the sour cream and vanilla extract.

5. Sift the remaining flour and cinnamon, the baking powder, baking soda, and salt into the creamed mixture and fold in gently.

6. Stir in the warm apples, then spoon the mixture into the prepared pan and smooth the surface. Sprinkle over the reserved crumb topping. Bake in the oven for 40–45 minutes, or until a skewer inserted into the center comes out clean. Turn out onto a wire rack and leave to cool. Serve in slices.

GOOSEBERRY & ELDERFLOWER Cake

A lovely moist cake that can also be served warm as a dessert. For a change, try using cooked plums, apples, or rhubarb instead of gooseberries.

MAKES: 8–10 SLICES

2 cups self-rising flour
1 teaspoon baking powder
1/2 cup superfine sugar
1/2 cup light brown sugar
1/2 cup/ 1 stick unsalted butter, melted
2 eggs, beaten
1 1/4 cups cooked unsweetened gooseberries
2 tablespoons elderflower cordial

FOR THE ICING
1 cup icing sugar, sifted
3–5 teaspoons elderflower cordial

1. Preheat the oven to 350°F. Grease and line a 9-inch springform pan fitted with a flat base.

2. For the cake, mix the flour, baking powder and sugars together in a bowl. Add the melted butter and eggs and mix well. Stir in the gooseberries and elderflower cordial until well combined. Spoon the mixture into the prepared pan and smooth the surface.

3. Bake in the oven for about 45 minutes, or until a skewer inserted into the center comes out clean. Cool in the pan for 5 minutes, then turn out onto a wire rack and leave to cool completely.

4. When the cake is cold, make the icing. Put the icing sugar in a bowl and stir in just enough elderflower cordial to make a thick pouring consistency. Using a teaspoon, drizzle the icing randomly and decoratively over the top of the cake. Serve in slices.

STRAWBERRY Shortcake

This classic summer recipe is sure to be a family favorite.

MAKES: **8 SLICES**

2²/₃ cups self-rising flour

1¹/₂ tablespoons baking powder

¹/₄ teaspoon salt

Generous 3 tablespoons/²/₃ stick
    chilled unsalted butter, cut into
    small pieces

¹/₂ cup superfine sugar

1 cup buttermilk, plus extra for
    brushing

Granulated sugar, for sprinkling

FOR THE FILLING

1 cup heavy cream

2 tablespoons powdered sugar

¹/₂ teaspoon vanilla extract

1 pound strawberries, halved

1. Preheat the oven to 375°F. Grease and flour a baking sheet. Sift the flour, baking powder, and salt into a bowl. Rub in the butter until the mixture resembles fine breadcrumbs.

2. Combine 5 tablespoons of the superfine sugar and the buttermilk in a bowl, then add this to the flour mixture. Mix to form a smooth dough, but do not overwork at this stage. Turn the dough onto a lightly floured surface and divide into two balls, one slightly larger than the other. Roll out each ball of dough to form a round about 1 inch thick.

3. Place the dough rounds on the prepared baking sheet. Brush off any excess flour. Brush the tops with buttermilk and sprinkle with granulated sugar. Bake in the oven for 20–25 minutes, or until golden brown. Transfer to a wire rack and leave to cool completely.

4. For the filling, whip the cream in a bowl until soft peaks form, then whisk in the powdered sugar and vanilla extract, mixing well. Set aside.

5. Put the strawberries in a saucepan with 2 tablespoons of water and the remaining 3 tablespoons of caster sugar and heat gently for 2–3 minutes to soften the fruit. Remove the pan from the heat.

6. Spoon the whipped cream onto the larger of the cooled shortcake rounds and spoon over the warm strawberries and juice. Top with the second shortcake round and serve immediately.

BRAIDED FRUIT Loaf

This is an unusual and beautiful loaf. Vary the fruit and alcohol according to taste—substitute all vine fruits, for example, or use brandy instead of rum.

MAKES: 6-8 SLICES

6 ounces mixed dried fruit, e.g. pineapple, raisins, golden raisins, mixed peel, candied cherries, roughly chopped
4 tablespoons rum
1²/₃ cup bread flour
¹/₂ teaspoon salt
1¹/₂ teaspoons active dried yeast
2 tablespoons light brown sugar
Scant ¹/₂ cup warmed milk
1 egg, beaten
¹/₄ cup ready-made marzipan, grated
6 tablespoons apricot jelly
1 tablespoon unsalted butter
1 tablespoon superfine sugar
1 tablespoon clear honey

1. Put the mixed dried fruit in a bowl and stir in the rum. Cover and leave to soak overnight.

2. Combine the flour, salt, yeast, and brown sugar in a bowl. Make a well in the center and add the milk and egg. Mix to a soft dough, then knead for about 10 minutes, or until smooth. Shape into a ball and put into a clean oiled bowl. Cover and leave to rise in a warm place for about 1 hour, or until doubled in size.

3. Meanwhile, mix the soaked fruit, marzipan, and apricot jelly together. Preheat the oven to 400°F. Grease a baking sheet. Knead the dough again briefly for about 1 minute on a lightly floured surface, then roll out to form a 12 x 14-inch rectangle. Trim to a neat shape.

4. Spread the fruit mixture in a 3 inch strip down the center of the rectangle leaving a margin of 2 inches at each end. Make diagonal cuts, each about ³/₄-inch wide in the dough down either side of the filling.

5. Fold the strips of dough up over the filling, overlapping alternate strips. Tuck in the two ends. Transfer to the prepared baking sheet. Cover with oiled plastic wrap and leave to rise for 20 minutes.

6. Meanwhile, melt the butter, superfine sugar, and honey together in a small saucepan, then brush this mixture evenly over the braided loaf. Bake in the oven for 20–25 minutes, or until golden brown. Transfer to a wire rack to cool. Serve in slices.

CARAMEL PECAN Loaf

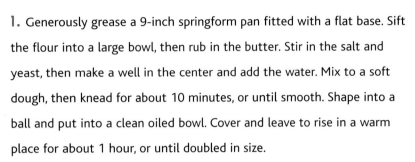

MAKES: 8–10 SLICES

3¼ cups bread flour
1 tablespoon unsalted butter
2 teaspoons salt
1½ teaspoons active dried yeast
1¼ cups warmed water

PECAN FILLING & TOPPING
¾ cup/1½ sticks unsalted butter
⅔ cup light brown sugar
1 cup pecans, roughly chopped
2 tablespoons heavy cream

1. Generously grease a 9-inch springform pan fitted with a flat base. Sift the flour into a large bowl, then rub in the butter. Stir in the salt and yeast, then make a well in the center and add the water. Mix to a soft dough, then knead for about 10 minutes, or until smooth. Shape into a ball and put into a clean oiled bowl. Cover and leave to rise in a warm place for about 1 hour, or until doubled in size.

2. Knead the dough again briefly for about 1 minute on a lightly floured surface, then pat out to form a 10 x 14-inch rectangle. Trim to a neat shape. Cover and leave to rest for 10 minutes. Preheat the oven to 400°F.

3. Meanwhile, cream ½ cup of the butter and ½ cup of the sugar together in a bowl until smooth. Stir in most of the pecans. Spread the mixture evenly over the dough, leaving a 1 inch margin around the edges. Starting from a long side, roll up the dough tightly and cut into 2 inch slices. Arrange the slices in the prepared pan, cut-side up. Cover and leave to rise for about 30 minutes, or until the dough has risen to the top of the pan.

4. Bake the loaf in the oven for 30–40 minutes, or until risen and golden brown, covering the top with foil if it begins to over-brown.

5. Meanwhile, melt the remaining butter and sugar together in a saucepan over a low heat. Add the cream and bring to the boil. Simmer for 3–4 minutes, then add the remaining pecans and cook for 1 minute. Remove from the heat.

6. Remove the loaf from the oven and immediately spread the pecan mixture evenly over the top. Cool in the pan, then turn out and serve in slices.

ALMOND MACAROON Cake

A simple fruit cake with an unusual almond macaroon topping. This cake improves if kept wrapped in foil for a couple of days before cutting.

MAKES: **10 SLICES**

¾ cup/1½ sticks unsalted butter, softened

¾ cup superfine sugar

3 eggs, beaten

1 egg yolk

1½ cups all-purpose flour

1 teaspoon almond extract

¾ cup chopped mixed citrus peel

¾ cup golden raisins

¾ cup raisins

1 cup natural-color candied cherries, halved

FOR THE TOPPING

1 egg white

½ cup superfine sugar

¾ cup ground almonds

½ teaspoon almond extract

2–3 tablespoons sliced almonds

1. Preheat the oven to 325°F. Grease the bottom and sides of a deep 8-inch round cake pan and double-line with non-stick baking paper.

2. For the cake, beat the butter and sugar together in a bowl until light and fluffy. Gradually beat in the eggs and egg yolk, adding a little flour if the mixture begins to curdle.

3. Fold in the remaining flour and the almond extract. Add the mixed peel, golden raisins, raisins, and candied cherries, mixing well. Turn the mixture into the prepared pan and smooth the surface. Set aside.

4. For the topping, whisk the egg white in a bowl until light and fluffy but not stiff. Whisk in the sugar, then fold in the ground almonds and almond extract. Spread this almond mixture evenly over the top of the cake mixture in the pan. Sprinkle with the flaked almonds.

5. Place in the oven and put a baking sheet on top of the cake pan to cover it completely. Bake for 1¼–1½ hours, or until a skewer inserted into the center comes out clean. Remove the cake from the oven and remove the baking sheet. Leave the cake to cool in the pan, then carefully turn out and serve in slices.

FRUIT Gingerbread

Everyone will enjoy this afternoon treat—it's really a cross between a cake and a quickbread, and it is delicious served sliced with butter.

MAKES: 6–8 SQUARES

3 1/2 cups all-purpose flour
1 teaspoon baking powder
1 tablespoon ground ginger
1 teaspoon ground cinnamon
1 cup/2 sticks unsalted butter
1/2 cup molasses
3/4 cup light brown sugar
3 eggs, beaten
3 ounces dried cherries, halved
4 ounces pitted dried dates, chopped
2 ounces preserved candied ginger, drained and chopped
3/4 cup golden raisins

1. Preheat the oven to 300°F. Grease and line a deep 8-inch square cake pan.

2. Mix the flour, baking powder, ground ginger, and cinnamon in a large bowl. Set aside. Place the butter in a saucepan with the molasses and sugar and stir over a low heat until melted. Pour into the flour mixture and mix well. Beat in the eggs until smooth, then stir in the dried cherries, dates, candied ginger, and golden raisins, mixing well.

3. Pour the mixture evenly into the prepared pan. Bake in the oven for 1–1 1/4 hours, or until a skewer inserted into the center comes out clean. Cool in the pan for 10 minutes, then turn out onto a wire rack and leave to cool completely. Serve in slices or squares.

APPLE & RASPBERRY Cake

This delicious moist sponge is ideal for lunchboxes or picnics.

MAKES: 6–8 SQUARES

⅔ cup/1¼ sticks unsalted butter, chopped

1 cup superfine sugar

2 eggs, lightly beaten

1 teaspoon vanilla essence

Generous 1 cup self-rising flour, sifted

¾ cup vanilla-flavored yogurt

1 large apple, peeled, cored, and grated

⅔ cup raspberries

Sifted powdered sugar, for dusting

1. Preheat the oven to 350°F. Grease and line an 8-inch round cake pan.

2. Beat the butter and sugar together in a bowl until pale and fluffy. Gradually add the eggs, beating well after each addition. Stir in the vanilla essence. Add the flour, then the yogurt, grated apple, and raspberries and mix until smooth.

3. Spoon the mixture into the prepared pan and smooth the surface. Bake in the oven for 1 hour, or until golden and the center of the cake springs back when lightly pressed.

4. Leave in the pan for 30 minutes before turning out onto a wire rack to cool completely. Dust with powdered sugar before serving.

CAKE TIP

Instead of apples and raspberries try using pear and blueberries or blackberries as an alternative.

RICH BUTTER Cake

Use the best-quality ingredients you can for this loaf cake
and you'll taste the difference.

MAKES: 10–12 SLICES

1²/₃ cups self-rising flour
1 teaspoon baking powder
1 cup/2¼ sticks unsalted butter,
   softened
1 cup superfine sugar
3 eggs, beaten
3 tablespoons lowfat milk
1 teaspoon vanilla extract

CAKE TIP
*For a crunchy top,
scatter roughly
crushed sugar cubes on
top of the cake
before baking.*

1. Preheat the oven to 350°F. Grease and line a 10-inch loaf pan.

2. Sift the flour and baking powder into a bowl. Set aside. Cream the butter and sugar together in a separate bowl and beat for 4–5 minutes, or until pale and fluffy. Gradually beat in the eggs, milk, and vanilla extract, then fold in the flour until well mixed. Spoon the mixture into the prepared pan and level the surface.

3. Bake in the oven for 50–55 minutes, or until firm to the touch and a skewer inserted into the center comes out clean. Cool in the pan for 10 minutes, then turn out onto a wire rack and leave to cool completely. Serve in slices.

TROPICAL FRUIT Cake

To make this cake more decorative, reserve some of the chopped tropical fruit and sprinkle it over the top of the cake mixture just before baking.

MAKES: 8–10 SLICES

¾ cup/1½ sticks unsalted butter, softened
¾ cup superfine sugar
2 eggs, beaten
1¼ cup self-rising flour
2 tablespoons coconut cream
9 ounces mixed dried tropical fruit, chopped
⅓ cup macadamia nuts, chopped

1. Preheat the oven to 350°F. Grease and line a 5-inch loaf pan.

2. Beat the butter and sugar together in a bowl until light and fluffy. Gradually add the eggs, beating well after each addition. Fold in the flour, then stir in the coconut cream.

3. Stir in the tropical fruit and macadamia nuts. Spoon the mixture into the prepared pan and smooth the surface.

4. Bake in the oven for about 50 minutes, or until a skewer inserted into the center comes out clean. Cool in the pan for 5–10 minutes, then turn out onto a wire rack and leave to cool completely. Serve in slices.

CHOCOLATE REFRIGERATOR Cake

Refrigerator cakes are always a great favorite with adults and kids alike. This one is simple and quick to make and you can substitute any preferred fruits, if you like.

MAKES: 12–14 SLICES

1 pound dark bitter chocolate, broken into squares

1¼ cup/2¼ sticks unsalted butter

12 ounces shortbread cookies or graham crackers, roughly chopped

2 cups pecans, chopped

1 cup raisins

1 cup red candied cherries, halved

1 handful mini marshmallows

1. Grease and line a 10-inch loaf pan with a double layer of plastic wrap.

2. Melt the chocolate and butter together in a large heat-proof mixing bowl set over a pan of gently simmering water. Remove the bowl from the heat. Add all the remaining ingredients and stir together until well mixed.

3. Spoon the mixture into the prepared pan and smooth the surface. Cover and refrigerate for 2–3 hours, or until firm enough to turn out. Serve in slices.

CAKE TIP

You can substitute ginger snaps or any other favorite cookies for those used in this recipe if prefered.

AFTERNOON
TEA

CHERRY LOAF Cake

Here is a loaf cake that is quick and simple to make—the perfect
cake to bake in a hurry if unexpected guests stop by.

MAKES: 10–12 SLICES

1½ cups all-purpose flour
1 teaspoon baking powder
1¼ cups/2 sticks unsalted butter,
   softened
1 cup superfine sugar
3 eggs, beaten
3 tablespoons lowfat milk
1 teaspoon vanilla extract
½ cup ground almonds
1 cup candied cherries, cut in half

1. Preheat the oven to 350°F. Grease and line a 10-inch loaf pan.

2. Sift the flour and baking powder into a bowl. In a separate bowl,
cream the butter and sugar together until pale and fluffy. Gradually beat
in the eggs, milk, and vanilla extract until well combined. Fold in the flour,
ground almonds, and candied cherries.

3. Spoon the mixture into the prepared pan and smooth the surface.
Bake in the oven for 50–55 minutes, or until firm to the touch and a
skewer inserted into the center comes out clean. Cool in the pan for
10 minutes, then turn out onto a wire rack and leave to cool completely.

CAKE TIP
*To stop candied
cherries sinking, wash
and pat them dry
before using.*

CINNAMON SWIRL Bread

MAKES: 10–12 SLICES

5 cups bread flour

½ cup sugar

1 teaspoon salt

2 teaspoons fast-action dried yeast

¾ cup/1¼ unsalted butter

1¾ cups milk

2 eggs, beaten

4 heaping tablespoons light brown
   sugar

2 teaspoons ground cinnamon

Sifted powdered sugar, to decorate

1. Place the flour, sugar, and salt in a large bowl, then stir in the yeast. Make a well in the center of the mixture.

2. Melt the butter in a saucepan. Add the milk to the melted butter and heat until it is just warm or hot to the touch. Pour the mixture into the well in the flour, add the eggs, and mix together with a wooden spoon until you have a smooth dough.

3. Cover the dough and leave to rise in a warm place for 45–60 minutes, or until it has doubled in size. Meanwhile, mix the brown sugar with the cinnamon and set aside. Grease a 2½ quart (10 cup) Kugelhopf pan.

4. Beat the dough with a wooden spoon to knock it back. With well-floured hands, divide the dough into four equal pieces.

5. Place a piece of dough in the prepared pan and stretch it around the base until it is covered. Sprinkle over a quarter of the cinnamon sugar mixture. Take a second piece of dough and stretch it over the first one. Sprinkle with cinnamon sugar. Repeat twice more. Leave to rise for 15 minutes. Meanwhile preheat the oven to 425°F.

6. Bake the loaf in the oven for 20 minutes, then reduce the oven temperature to 375°F and bake for a further 5–10 minutes, or until the bread is risen and sounds hollow when tapped underneath. Turn out onto a wire rack and leave to cool. Dredge the bread with sifted powdered sugar and serve in slices.

JELLY ROLL with Lemon Cream

MAKES: 6–8 SLICES

4 large eggs
½ cup superfine sugar, plus extra for
    dusting
⅔ cup all-purpose flour
Sifted powdered sugar and finely
    grated lemon zest, to decorate

FOR THE FILLING
2½ cups mascarpone cheese
Finely grated zest and juice of
    ½ lemon
2 tablespoons freshly squeezed
    orange juice
4 tablespoons powdered sugar

1. Preheat the oven to 425°F. Grease and line a 10 x 15 inch jelly roll pan.

2. For the sponge, using a hand-held electric mixer, whisk the eggs and sugar together in a large bowl until the mixture is pale, creamy, and thick enough to leave a trail on the surface when the whisk is lifted.

3. Sift and fold in the flour in three batches. Pour the mixture into the prepared pan, tilting the pan backwards and forwards to spread evenly. Bake in the oven for about 10 minutes, or until risen and golden brown, and the cake springs back when lightly pressed.

4. While the cake is cooking, lay a sheet of greaseproof paper on a work surface and sprinkle liberally with superfine sugar.

5. Quickly turn the hot cake out onto the sugar-dusted paper and remove the lining paper. Trim off the crusty edges, score a cut half an inch in from one of the shorter ends, then roll up the cake from the scored short end with the paper inside. Place on a wire rack and leave to cool.

6. For the filling, put all the filling ingredients in a bowl and beat together until smooth and well mixed. Carefully unroll the cake, remove the paper, and spread the filling mixture evenly over the cake. Re-roll the cake. To decorate, dredge the cake with sifted powdered sugar and sprinkle with lemon zest.

CARIBBEAN BANANA Bread

A great way to use up over-ripe bananas that no one wants to eat—
they are transformed into a delicious, moist, and spicy cake.

MAKES: 6–8 SLICES

2 bananas, peeled
2 tablespoons clear honey
1½ cups self-rising flour
½ teaspoon baking powder
1 teaspoon freshly grated nutmeg
¾ cup/1⅓ sticks unsalted butter,
   softened
Generous ½ cup light brown sugar
2 eggs, beaten
⅓ cup pecans, finely chopped

1. Preheat the oven to 350°F. Grease and line an 8½-inch loaf pan.

2. Mash the bananas in a bowl with the honey. Sift the flour, baking powder, and nutmeg into a separate bowl.

3. Cream the butter and sugar together in a large mixing bowl until pale and fluffy, then gradually add the eggs, beating well after each addition.

4. Fold in the bananas and the flour mixture together with the pecans. Spoon the mixture into the prepared pan and smooth the surface. Bake in the oven for 50–60 minutes, or until risen and golden brown, and a skewer inserted into the center comes out clean.

5. Cool in the pan for 10 minutes, then turn out onto a wire rack and leave to cool completely.

ORANGE & ALMOND
Sponge Cake

This moist iced sponge cake is a great accompaniment to morning coffee or afternoon tea and it is special enough for dessert, too.

MAKES: 6–8 SLICES

¾ cup/1½ sticks unsalted butter
Scant 1 cup superfine sugar
3 eggs, beaten
1 cup self-rising flour
½ cup ground almonds
Few drops of almond extract
Toasted sliced almonds and thinly
   pared orange zest, to decorate

FOR THE FROSTING
1¼ cups cream cheese
2 tablespoons freshly squeezed
   orange juice
2 teaspoons finely grated orange zest
Scant 1 cup powdered sugar, sifted

1. Preheat the oven to 375°F. Grease and line two 8-inch round cake pans.

2. For the cake, beat the butter and sugar together in a bowl until pale and fluffy. Gradually add the eggs, beating well after each addition. Sift the flour over the creamed mixture, then gently fold in with the ground almonds and almond extract until well combined.

3. Spoon the mixture into the prepared pans, dividing it evenly, then smooth the surface. Bake in the oven for 20–25 minutes, or until risen and golden brown and the centers of the cakes spring back when lightly pressed. Turn out onto a wire rack and leave to cool.

4. Meanwhile, make the frosting. Beat the cream cheese in a bowl to soften. Add the orange juice, orange zest, and powdered sugar and beat together until smooth and creamy.

5. Sandwich the two cakes together with a little frosting, then spread the remaining frosting over the top of the cake. Scatter with toasted, sliced almonds and orange zest to decorate.

AMERICAN WHISKED
Sponge Cake

This traditional light-as-a-feather sponge cake is flavored with vanilla and is perfect served with fruit and cream for afternoon tea.

MAKES: 6–8 SLICES

3 large eggs, separated
½ cup superfine sugar
1 teaspoon vanilla extract
¼ teaspoon cream of tartar
⅔ cup all-purpose flour, sifted
Pinch of salt
1⅓ cup heavy cream
3½ ounces fresh strawberries
Sifted powdered sugar, for dusting

1. Preheat the oven to 350°F. Grease and line two 8-inch round cake pans.

2. Using a hand-held electric mixer, whisk the egg yolks and ¼ cup of the superfine sugar together in a bowl until the mixture is pale and creamy. Whisk in the vanilla extract. Set aside.

3. In a separate bowl, whisk the egg whites and cream of tartar together until they are stiff. Gradually whisk in the remaining superfine sugar until the mixture is stiff and glossy. Sift the flour and salt over the egg yolk mixture and fold in with a quarter of the whisked egg whites. Fold in the remaining whisked egg whites.

4. Pour the mixture into the prepared pans, dividing it evenly. Bake in the oven for about 30 minutes, or until golden brown and the tops spring back when lightly pressed. Turn out onto a wire rack and leave to cool.

5. Whip the cream in a bowl to form soft peaks. Chop all but 1–2 strawberries. Sandwich the cakes together with the whipped cream and chopped strawberries. Dust the top of the cake with sifted powdered sugar and decorate with small whole or halved strawberries.

SIMPLE ALMOND Cake

This light and simple cake packed with ground almonds is delicious served with fresh fruit and whipped cream for a filling afternoon treat.

MAKES: 8–10 SLICES

2 tablespoons all-purpose flour, sifted
2½ cups ground almonds
7 large egg whites
1 cup superfine sugar
2 tablespoons orange-flavored liqueur
Scant ⅔ cup whipping cream,
    whipped to form soft peaks
6 ounces strawberries, sliced
Sifted powdered sugar, for dusting

1. Preheat the oven to 350°F. Grease and line a 9-inch springform pan fitted with a flat base.

2. Sift the flour into a bowl, then stir in the ground almonds. Set aside. Whisk the egg whites in a separate bowl until stiff. Gradually whisk in the cup of superfine sugar, until the mixture is stiff and glossy.

3. Gently fold the flour and almond mixture into the whisked egg whites. Spoon the mixture into the prepared pan and smooth the surface. Bake in the oven for 25–30 minutes, or until golden brown and spongy to the touch.

4. Remove the cake from the oven and leave to cool completely in the pan, then turn out onto a board. Slice the cake in half horizontally, then drizzle the orange liqueur over each half. Spread one half of the cake, cut-side up, with the whipped cream and top with the sliced strawberries. Top with the second cake half, cut-side down, and dust with sifted powdered sugar. Serve in slices.

CAKE TIP
To prevent the cream becoming over-whipped, slightly under-whip the cream and then finish with a hand whisk or a very low speed on an electric mixer.

ANGEL FOOD Cake

A truly magnificent feat in the art of cake-making, this impressive cake is held together almost by air.

MAKES: 8–10 SLICES

$1/3$ cup all-purpose flour
1 tablespoon cornstarch
1 cup superfine sugar
7 egg whites
$3/4$ teaspoon cream of tartar
Pinch of salt
$1^1/2$ teaspoons vanilla extract
2 tablespoons toasted chopped pistachio nuts, to decorate

FOR THE FROSTING
2 egg whites
$2^1/3$ cups superfine sugar
$1/4$ teaspoon cream of tartar

1. Preheat the oven to 350°F. Grease and line a 9-inch springform pan fitted with a tube base.

2. For the cake, sift the flour and cornstarch into a bowl. Add $1/3$ cup of the sugar and sift together twice.

3. In a separate large bowl, whisk the egg whites until foamy. Add the cream of tartar and salt and whisk until stiff. Whisk the remaining sugar into the egg whites until the mixture is stiff and glossy. Whisk in the vanilla extract.

4. Carefully fold in the flour mixture, then spoon the batter into the prepared pan and smooth the surface. Bake in the oven for 45–50 minutes, or until pale golden and spongy to the touch. Place the cake pan on a wire rack and leave to cool in the pan.

5. To make the frosting, put all the frosting ingredients in a heat-proof bowl, add 4 tablespoons of water, and set the bowl over a pan of hot water. Using a hand-held electric mixer, whisk the mixture for 10–12 minutes, or until thick.

6. Run a knife around the inside edge of the pan and remove the cold cake. Spread the frosting evenly over the top and sides of the cake and finish with a sprinkling of toasted chopped pistachio nuts.

SPICED APPLE, CRANBERRY & CIDER Cake

This is an attractive cake, which is very fruity and not overly sweet. As it contains fresh fruit it is best eaten within a couple of days of making, or keep it refrigerated.

MAKES: 6–8 SLICES

3 medium red-skinned apples
¾ cup dried sweetened cranberries
¾ cup dry cider
2¾ cups self-rising flour
2 teaspoons ground cinnamon
¾ cup light brown sugar
¾ cup/1½ sticks unsalted butter, melted
3 eggs, beaten

FOR THE TOPPING
1 medium red-skinned apple, thinly sliced and seeds removed
3 tablespoons apricot jelly, warmed

1. For the cake, peel and core the apples, then chop them roughly. Put the apples, cranberries, and cider in a saucepan and bring to the boil, then simmer very gently for 5 minutes. Remove the pan from the heat and set aside to cool completely.

2. Preheat the oven to 350°F. Grease and line a 8-inch springform pan fitted with a flat base.

3. Sift the flour and cinnamon into a bowl and stir in the sugar. Add the melted butter, eggs, apples, and cider mixture. Stir until just combined, then spoon into the prepared pan and smooth the surface. For the topping, arrange the apple slices evenly over the top of the cake mixture.

4. Bake in the oven for 50–60 minutes, or until a skewer inserted into the center comes out clean. Leave to cool in the pan for 5 minutes, then turn out onto a wire rack.

5. Brush the apricot jelly over the top of the cake while it is still warm. Leave to cool completely, then serve in slices.

GOLDEN BUTTERCREAM Cake

Rich and buttery, this cake is an anytime cake. Eat and enjoy!

MAKES: 6–8 SLICES

1²/₃ cups self-rising flour
2 teaspoons baking powder
Pinch of salt
1 cup/2 sticks unsalted butter,
    softened
1¼ cups superfine sugar
4 eggs, beaten
1 teaspoon vanilla extract

FOR THE FROSTING
½ cup/1 stick unsalted butter,
    softened
1 teaspoon vanilla extract
Scant 2 cups powdered sugar, sifted
3–4 drops of yellow food coloring

1. Preheat the oven to 350°F. Grease and line two 8-inch round cake pans.

2. For the cake, sift the flour, baking powder, and salt into a bowl. In a separate bowl, beat the butter until pale and fluffy. Add the sugar and beat for a further 2 minutes. Gradually add the eggs, beating well after each addition. Add the vanilla extract, then fold in the flour mixture.

3. Spoon the mixture into the prepared pans, dividing it evenly, and smooth the surface. Bake in the oven for 30–35 minutes, or until risen, golden, and firm to the touch. Turn out onto a wire rack and leave to cool.

4. For the frosting, beat the butter and vanilla extract together in a bowl until pale and fluffy, then stir in the powdered sugar. Add the yellow food coloring and beat to mix well. Sandwich the two cakes together with some frosting, then spread the remaining frosting over the top of the cake.

FRUIT TEA Loaf

This recipe is incredibly easy to make, and the cake is a great standby in case family or friends visit. It's delicious served in slices spread with butter.

MAKES: 8–10 SLICES

2 cups mixed dried fruit, such as
    golden raisins, currants, raisins, and
    candied cherries
Generous ½ cup light brown sugar
½ cup/1 stick unsalted butter
⅔ cup brewed tea
2 teaspoons ground allspice
Finely grated zest of 1 orange
2 cups self-rising flour, sifted
1 tablespoon clear honey, warmed

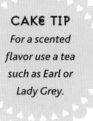

CAKE TIP
*For a scented
flavor use a tea
such as Earl or
Lady Grey.*

1. Place the mixed dried fruit, sugar, butter, tea, and allspice in a saucepan. Cover and heat gently until the butter has melted, stirring occasionally. Bring to the boil and boil for 1 minute, then remove the pan from the heat. Add the orange zest, then set aside and leave overnight.

2. Preheat the oven to 350°F. Grease and line a 8½-inch loaf tin.

3. Fold the sifted flour into the fruit mixture. Spoon the mixture into the prepared pan and smooth the surface. Bake in the oven for 50–55 minutes, or until golden brown and a skewer inserted into the center comes out clean.

4. Remove the cake from the oven, brush the top of the cake with warmed honey, then leave it to cool completely in the pan. Turn out and serve in slices spread with butter, if you like.

DATE & WALNUT Loaf

This is a lovely moist cake that slices well and
keeps for more than a week if wrapped in foil.

MAKES: 12–14 SLICES

½ cup/1 stick unsalted butter
½ cup light brown sugar
¼ cup light corn syrup
⅔ cup milk
2 large eggs, beaten
2 cups all-purpose flour
1 level teaspoon baking soda
1 teaspoon ground pumpkin pie spice
¾ cup pitted dried dates, chopped
½ cup walnuts, chopped

FOR THE TOPPING
¼ cup pitted dried dates, chopped
¼ cup walnuts, chopped
1 tablespoon superfine sugar
1 teaspoon ground cinnamon

1. Preheat the oven to 300°F. Grease and line a 10-inch loaf pan.

2. For the cake, put the butter, sugar, and corn syrup in a large saucepan and heat gently, stirring. When the butter has melted, remove the pan from the heat and set aside to cool for a few minutes.

3. Stir the milk and eggs into the syrup mixture. Sift the flour, baking soda, and mixed spice into a bowl, then stir in the syrup mixture. Mix to a smooth batter, then fold in the dates and walnuts.

4. Pour the mixture evenly into the prepared pan. Mix the topping ingredients together and sprinkle thickly over the top of the cake.

5. Bake in the oven for 1–1¼ hours, or until a skewer inserted into the center comes out clean. Cool in the pan for 5 minutes, then turn out onto a wire rack and leave to cool completely. Serve in slices.

ORANGE CHIFFON Cake

Light and flavorful, this citrus cake is delicious served on its own or with some fruit for a tempting afternoon treat.

MAKES: 12–14 SLICES

1½ cups self-rising flour
2 teaspoons baking powder
Pinch of salt
1½ cups superfine sugar
½ cup safflower or sunflower oil
3 eggs, separated
¾ cup unsweetened orange juice
2 tablespoons finely grated
   orange zest
1 teaspoon vanilla extract
Pinch of cream of tartar

1. Preheat the oven to 325°F. Grease a-10 inch Bundt tin.

2. Combine the flour, baking powder, salt, and sugar in a bowl. Make a well in the center of the dry ingredients and add the oil, egg yolks, orange juice, orange zest, and vanilla extract. Beat together for about 1 minute, or until smooth.

3. In a separate bowl, whisk the egg whites until they start to form soft peaks. Add the cream of tartar and whisk until stiff peaks form. Fold the whisked egg whites into the cake mixture using a balloon whisk.

4. Pour the mixture evenly into the prepared pan. Bake in the oven for 55 minutes, or until firm to the touch. Invert the cake onto a wire rack, but leave to cool in the pan. Run a knife around the inside edges of the pan and remove the cold cake. Serve in slices.

GERMAN CHOCOLATE Cake

A rich and buttery, nutty icing works well with this light chocolate sponge, which is ideal for sharing with friends.

MAKES: 8–10 SLICES

4 ounces dark bitter chocolate
³/₄ cup/1¹/₂ sticks unsalted butter
1¹/₂ cups superfine sugar
3 eggs, beaten
1¹/₂ cups self-rising flour
1 teaspoon baking soda
Pinch of salt
1 cup buttermilk

FOR THE FILLING
1¹/₂ cups evaporated milk
1¹/₂ cups superfine sugar
³/₄ cup/1¹/₂ sticks unsalted butter
4 egg yolks
2 teaspoons vanilla extract
7 ounces sweetened flaked or dried
   coconut
1¹/₂ cups pecans, chopped

1. Preheat the oven to 350°F. Grease and line three 8-inch round cake pans.

2. For the cake, melt the chocolate and butter in a large heat-proof bowl set over a pan of gently simmering water. Stir to melt the chocolate, then stir in the sugar. Remove from the heat, then using a hand-held electric mixer, gradually beat in the eggs using a low speed.

3. Beat in ¹/₃ cup of the flour, the baking soda, and salt. Add the remaining flour alternately with the buttermilk. Beat well for 1 minute to produce a smooth batter.

4. Divide the mixture between the prepared pans, dividing it evenly, then smooth the surface. Bake in the oven for 25–30 minutes, or until risen and just firm to the touch. Turn out onto a wire rack and leave to cool.

5. For the filling, pour the evaporated milk into a saucepan and add the sugar, butter, egg yolks, and vanilla extract. Cook over a medium heat for 10–12 minutes, stirring continuously. The mixture will thicken and turn golden brown. Remove the pan from the heat, strain the mixture through a strainer, then stir in the coconut and pecans. Cool the mixture to room temperature before using it to sandwich together and cover the three sponge cakes. Serve in slices.

SIMPLE RAISIN FRUIT Cake

Ground allspice and vanilla extract flavour this sumptuous raisin cake—perfect served with morning coffee or afternoon tea.

MAKES: 12–14 SLICES

1²/₃ cups all-purpose flour
1 teaspoon baking powder
1 cup/2 sticks unsalted butter, softened
1 cup superfine sugar
3 eggs, beaten
3 tablespoons lowfat milk
1 teaspoon vanilla extract
½ teaspoon ground allspice
1 cup raisins
Sifted powdered sugar, to dust

1. Preheat the oven to 350°F. Grease and line a 10-inch loaf pan.

2. Sift the flour and baking powder into a bowl. In a separate bowl, cream the butter and superfine sugar together until pale and fluffy. Gradually beat in the eggs, milk, and vanilla extract until well combined. Fold in the flour, allspice and raisins.

3. Spoon the mixture into the prepared pan and smooth the surface. Bake in the oven for 50–55 minutes, or until firm to the touch and a skewer inserted into the center comes out clean.

4. Cool in the pan for 10 minutes, then turn out onto a wire rack and leave to cool completely. Dust lightly with powdered sugar and serve in slices.

CAKE TIP
To make this cake even more delicious, soak the raisins overnight in the juice of 1 orange.

POUND CAKE
with Butter Syrup

Pound cake is a very old recipe originally using a pound of each ingredient—
butter, sugar, eggs, and flour. This scaled-down version has a wonderful butter glaze.

MAKES: 16–20 SLICES

1½ cups/3 sticks unsalted butter,
    softened
1½ cups superfine sugar
2 teaspoons finely grated lemon zest
1½ cups plain flour
1 cup potato flour
1½ teaspoons baking powder
6 eggs, beaten
2 tablespoons milk

FOR THE GLAZE
½ cup superfine sugar
¼ cup/½ stick unsalted butter
1 teaspoon vanilla extract

1. Preheat the oven to 350°F. Prepare a 10-inch Bundt pan by brushing it twice with melted butter and dusting lightly with flour.

2. For the cake, beat the butter and sugar together in a bowl until pale and fluffy. Stir in the lemon zest. In a separate bowl, sift together the plain flour, potato flour, and baking powder.

3. Gradually beat the eggs into the creamed mixture, adding a little of the flour if the mixture begins to curdle. Fold in the remaining flour mixture, then stir in the milk until well mixed. Spoon the mixture into the prepared pan and smooth the surface.

4. Bake in the oven for 45–55 minutes, or until a skewer inserted into the center comes out clean. Remove the cake from the oven and ease it away from the sides of the pan. Leave to cool in the pan for 10 minutes before turning out onto a wire rack.

5. To make the glaze, put the sugar, butter, and 4 tablespoons of water in a saucepan and heat gently, stirring until the butter has melted. Simmer gently for 3 minutes, then remove the pan from the heat and stir in the vanilla extract. Pour the butter glaze evenly over the warm cake and leave to cool completely. Serve in slices.

CHOCOLATE Layer Cake

MAKES: 10 SLICES

2 cups all-purpose flour

1½ teaspoons baking soda

½ teaspoon baking powder

1 teaspoon salt

1½ cups superfine sugar

2 teaspoons vanilla extract

1¼ cups buttermilk

½ cup margarine

3 eggs

3 ounces plain chocolate, melted and cooled

Chocolate leaves or curls, to decorate (optional)

FOR THE FUDGY FROSTING

2 cups heavy cream

1 pound good-quality semi-sweet or dark bitter chocolate, chopped

⅓ cup unsalted butter, at room temperature

1 tablespoon vanilla extract

CAKE TIP

For a four-layer cake, slice the two cakes in half horizontally and frost between each layer, ending with the last layer of cake flat-side up, then frost the top and sides of the cake as above.

1. Preheat the oven to 350°F. Grease and flour two 10-inch round cake pans.

2. Sift the flour, baking soda, baking powder, and salt into a large mixing bowl. Add the sugar, vanilla extract, buttermilk, margarine, eggs, and cooled melted chocolate. Using a hand-held electric mixer on low speed, begin to beat the mixture slowly until the ingredients are well blended, then increase the mixer speed to high and beat for 5 minutes, scraping down the sides of the bowl occasionally.

3. Spoon the mixture into the prepared pans, dividing it evenly, then level the surface. Bake in the oven for about 25 minutes, or until the tops of the cakes are set. A skewer inserted into the center should come out with just one or two crumbs attached. Cool in the pans for 10 minutes, then turn out onto a wire rack and leave to cool completely.

4. To make the frosting, pour the cream into a saucepan and bring to a boil over a medium-high heat. Remove the pan from the heat and add the chocolate, stirring until melted and smooth. Beat in the butter and vanilla extract until well combined. Chill in the refrigerator, stirring every 10–15 minutes, until the frosting becomes quite thick and spreadable. Remove from the refrigerator and continue to stir occasionally until the frosting is thick.

5. Place one cake, top-side up, on a plate and spread evenly with about a quarter of the chocolate frosting. Place the second cake on top, flat-side up, then spread the top and sides of the cake with the remaining frosting, making deep swirls with a palette knife or the back of a spoon. Decorate with chocolate leaves or curls, if using. Serve in slices.

CARROT & BRAZIL NUT Cake

This is a very easy cake to make and it is equally good with or without the frosting. It makes a healthy addition to a packed lunch.

MAKES: 18 SQUARES

Generous 2 cups self-rising flour
1½ cups superfine sugar
2 teaspoons baking powder
1 cup Brazil nuts, chopped
2 teaspoons ground cinnamon
1 teaspoon ground ginger
1¼ cup sunflower oil
10½ ounces carrots, grated
4 eggs, beaten
1 teaspoon vanilla extract

FOR THE TOPPING
2 cups low-fat cream cheese
1 tablespoon clear honey
Brazil nuts, to decorate

1. Preheat the oven to 350°F. Grease and line a 9 x 11-inch cake tin.

2. For the cake, put the flour, sugar, baking powder, Brazil nuts, cinnamon, and ground ginger in a large bowl. Add the sunflower oil, grated carrots, eggs, and vanilla extract and beat together to mix well. Pour the mixture evenly into the prepared pan.

3. Bake in the oven for about 50 minutes, or until firm to the touch. Cool in the pan for 5–10 minutes, then turn out onto a wire rack and leave to cool completely.

4. For the topping, combine the cream cheese and honey in a bowl. Spread the topping mixture evenly over the top of the cake. Decorate with Brazil nuts and serve in slices or squares.

LEMON & GINGER Cake

This sharp-tasting, moist cake will keep well—if it lasts long enough!

MAKES: 12–14 SLICES

1²/₃ cups all-purpose flour
1 teaspoon baking powder
1¼ cups/2 sticks unsalted butter, softened
1 cup superfine sugar
3 eggs, beaten
3 tablespoons lowfat milk
½ cup ground almonds
1 teaspoon ground ginger
2 tablespoons finely grated lemon zest
2 tablespoons finely shredded candied lemon peel

1. Preheat the oven to 350°F. Grease and line a 10-inch loaf pan.

2. Sift the flour and baking powder into a bowl. In a separate bowl, cream the butter and sugar together until pale and fluffy. Gradually beat in the eggs and milk, then fold in the flour, ground almonds, ginger, and lemon zest.

3. Spoon the mixture into the prepared pan and smooth the surface. Bake in the oven for 55–60 minutes, or until firm to the touch and a skewer inserted into the center comes out clean.

4. Cool in the tin for 10 minutes, then turn out onto a wire rack and leave to cool completely. Spoon the candied lemon peel evenly over the top of the cake. Serve in slices.

CAKE TIP

To make your own candied peel, place pared strips of unwaxed lemon peel from 2 lemons in a small pan of water and bring to a boil. Drain and refresh under cold water. Repeat this process. Finely shred the peel, return it to the pan with enough water to cover and ½ cup superfine sugar. Heat gently to dissolve the sugar, then bring to a boil and simmer until the syrup thickens. Remove the pan from the heat and cool slightly. Spoon the candied peel over the top of the cake to decorate.

COFFEE, MAPLE & PECAN SPONGE Cake

MAKES: 6–8 SLICES

¹⁄₂ cup all-purpose flour
Pinch of salt
3 tablespoons unsalted butter
3 large eggs
6 tablespoons superfine sugar
1 teaspoon instant coffee powder
¹⁄₂ teaspoon vanilla extract
8 pecan halves, to decorate
FOR THE FROSTING
³⁄₄ cup/1¹⁄₄ sticks butter, softened
Scant 1 cup powdered sugar
1 teaspoon instant coffee powder
4 tablespoons maple syrup

1. Preheat the oven to 350°F. Grease and line a deep 8-inch round cake pan. For the cake, sift the flour and salt together three times into a bowl and set aside. Melt the butter and set aside.

2. Using a hand-held electric mixer, whisk the eggs and sugar together in a large, heat-proof bowl set over a pan of simmering water, until the mixture is pale, creamy, and thick enough to leave a trail on the surface when the whisk is lifted.

3. In a small bowl, dissolve the coffee in 1 tablespoon of hot water, then whisk this into the egg mixture together with the vanilla extract. Sift the flour over the egg mixture in three batches, drizzling a little melted butter around the edge of the mixture in between each batch, and carefully fold in.

4. Pour the mixture evenly into the prepared pan. Bake in the oven for 25–30 minutes, or until risen and golden. Cool in the pan for 2–3 minutes, then turn out onto a wire rack and leave to cool completely.

5. For the frosting, beat the butter and powdered sugar together in a bowl until smooth. In a small bowl, dissolve the coffee in 1 tablespoon of hot water, then gradually beat this into the creamed mixture together with the maple syrup until smooth and well mixed.

6. Cut the cake in half horizontally twice to make three layers. Sandwich the cake layers together with some of the frosting, then spread the remaining frosting over the top and sides of the cake. Decorate the top with pecan halves.

LEMON & LIME LOVE Cake

This tangy loaf cake is known by lots of different names, but Love Cake is particularly appropriate as everyone who tries it finds it impossible to resist!

MAKES: 12–14 SLICES

1¼ cups all-purpose flour
2 teaspoons baking powder
½ teaspoon salt
6 tablespoons unsalted butter, softened
1⅓ cups superfine sugar
2 eggs, lightly beaten
½ cup milk
Finely grated zest of 1 lemon and juice of ½ lemon
Finely grated zest and juice of 1 lime

1. Preheat the oven to 325°F. Grease and flour a 10-inch loaf pan. Sift the flour, baking powder, and salt into a large bowl.

2. Put the butter in a separate bowl and add scant 1 cup of the sugar. Beat together until pale and fluffy, then gradually beat in the eggs, adding a little flour if the mixture shows any sign of curdling. Gradually add the remaining flour, alternating with the milk and beating well after each addition. Stir in the lemon and lime zests.

3. Spoon the mixture into the prepared pan and smooth the surface. Bake in the oven for 40–50 minutes, or until a skewer inserted into the center comes out clean. Turn out onto a wire rack.

4. Mix the lemon and lime juices with the remaining sugar in a bowl. Put a tray underneath the wire rack and spoon the sugar mixture evenly over the top of the cake, letting it run down the sides slightly. Allow the cake to cool completely before serving in slices.

TURKISH FIG & SESAME Cake

A delicious cake packed with Middle Eastern flavors. It is ideal for lunch boxes, but it also makes a wonderful dessert when served with yogurt.

MAKES: 16 SQUARES

5 eggs, separated
1¼ cup superfine sugar
Finely grated zest of 1 lime
²/₃ cup semolina
1 cup ground almonds
1¹/₃ cups dried figs, chopped
2 tablespoons sesame seeds

FOR THE SYRUP
Juice of 2 limes
Scant ½ cup superfine sugar

1. Preheat the oven to 375°F. Grease and line a deep 9-inch square cake pan.

2. For the cake, using a hand-held electric mixer, whisk the egg yolks, sugar, and lime zest together in a bowl until the mixture is very thick and creamy. Fold in the semolina and ground almonds. In a separate bowl, whisk the egg whites until stiff, then fold one-third of the whisked whites into the almond mixture to loosen it. Fold in the remaining whisked egg whites until well combined.

3. Pour the mixture evenly into the prepared pan and sprinkle the chopped figs over the surface. Sprinkle the sesame seeds over the top. Bake in the oven for about 30 minutes, or until firm to the touch.

4. Meanwhile, make the syrup. Put the lime juice, 5 tablespoons of cold water, and the sugar in a saucepan and bring to a boil, stirring. Boil for about 2–3 minutes, or until syrupy. Remove the pan from the heat.

5. Remove the cake from the oven and prick the top surface all over with a toothpick or fork. Pour the hot syrup evenly over the hot cake, then leave the cake in the pan to cool completely. Once cold, turn out and serve in slices or squares.

BANOFFEE Cheesecake

MAKES: 10–12 SLICES

1½ cups all-purpose flour
Pinch of salt
7 tablespoons unsalted butter, diced
¼ cup superfine sugar

FOR THE FILLING

4 ounces dark bitter chocolate,
    broken into squares and melted
3 large ripe but firm bananas
Juice of ½ lemon
2½ cups mascarpone cheese
Scant ⅔ cup heavy cream, lightly
    whipped
1 10-ounce jar caramel sauce/spread

1. For the pastry, sift the flour into a bowl with the salt. Rub in the butter until the mixture resembles coarse breadcrumbs. Stir in the sugar. Add 3 tablespoons of cold water and mix to a dough. Turn the dough onto a lightly floured surface and knead briefly until the dough is smooth. Shape into a ball, wrap in plastic wrap and refrigerate for 20 minutes.

2. On a lightly floured surface, roll out the pastry to form a rough circle at least 2 inches larger than a loose-bottomed 9-inch fluted tart pan set on a baking sheet. Use the pastry circle to line the pan, pressing the pastry into the edges and trimming any overhanging pastry. Prick the base all over with a fork. Refrigerate for 20 minutes.

3. Meanwhile, preheat the oven to 400°F. Line the shell with greaseproof paper and pie weights and bake in the oven for 12 minutes. Remove the weights and paper and bake for a further 10–12 minutes, or until golden. Remove from the oven and set aside to cool.

4. Using a pastry brush, paint the melted chocolate onto the inside of the pastry shell to cover completely. Chill until set.

5. To assemble the cheesecake, peel and thickly slice the bananas, then toss them in the lemon juice. Set aside. Beat the mascarpone cheese in a bowl until softened, then stir in the whipped cream. Carefully fold the cream mixture and most of the caramel sauce together (reserving a little sauce for decoration), but don't over-mix—leave them marbled. Spoon the mixture evenly into the pastry case, then scatter the banana slices over the top. Drizzle the remaining caramel sauce decoratively over the bananas. Serve in slices.

LEMON & POPPY SEED POUND Cake

This poppy seed cake is soaked with a tangy lemon syrup after it has been baked to give a superbly moist texture and delicious taste. It will keep well in an airtight container for up to 1 week.

MAKES: 12–14 SLICES

¾ cup/1¼ sticks unsalted butter, softened
Scant 1 cup superfine sugar
3 eggs, beaten
Generous 1 cup self-rising flour
1 tablespoon poppy seeds
2 teaspoons finely grated lemon zest
FOR THE SYRUP
3 tablespoons granulated sugar
Juice of 1 lemon

1. Preheat the oven to 350°F. Grease and base line a 10-inch loaf pan.

2. For the cake, cream the butter and sugar together in a bowl until light and fluffy. Gradually beat in the eggs, beating well after each addition, then fold in the flour, poppy seeds, and lemon zest.

3. Turn the mixture into the prepared pan and smooth the surface. Bake in the oven for 1¼–1½ hours, or until risen and golden and a skewer inserted into the center comes out clean. Remove the cake from the oven but leave it in the pan.

4. To make the syrup, gently heat the sugar and lemon juice together in a saucepan, stirring until the sugar has dissolved. Bring to a boil, then remove the pan from the heat and pour the hot syrup over the hot cake. Leave the cake to cool completely in the pan, then turn out and serve in slices.

CAKE TIP

To squeeze the maximum juice from a lemon, make sure it is at room temperature and roll it under your palm on a work surface to soften the fruit and get the juices flowing.

PISTACHIO, YOGURT & CARDAMOM Cake

This cake has wonderful scented Middle Eastern flavors and is ideal for picnics and packed lunches.

MAKES: 6–8 SLICES

1½ cups pistachio nuts
Seeds from 8 cardamom pods, crushed
¾ cup unsalted butter
1 cup/1¼ sticks self-rising flour
Scant 1 cup superfine sugar
3 eggs, beaten
½ cup whole milk plain yogurt
1 teaspoon almond extract
Extra whole pistachio nuts, for decoration

1. Preheat the oven to 350°F. Grease and line a deep 8-inch round cake pan.

2. Put the pistachio nuts and cardamom seeds in a blender or food processor and process until finely chopped. Add the butter, flour, and sugar and pulse for about 20 seconds. Add the eggs, yogurt, and almond extract and pulse until just combined.

3. Spoon the mixture into the prepared pan and smooth the surface. Sprinkle the whole pistachio nuts over the top.

4. Bake in the oven for about 45–60 minutes, or until well risen, firm to the touch, and a skewer inserted into the center comes out clean. Cool in the pan for 5–10 minutes, then turn out onto a wire rack and leave to cool completely. Serve in slices.

CAKE TIP
To bring out the flavor of pistachios, spread them on a baking sheet and toast them in an oven preheated to 300°F for 5–10 minutes until just fragrant.

CHERRY Cheesecake

MAKES: 10–12 SLICES

2 cups all-purpose flour, sifted

Scant 1 cup powdered sugar

Generous 1/2 cup/1 1/3 sticks unsalted
   butter

6 egg yolks

2 teaspoons finely grated lemon zest

2 tablespoons heavy whipping cream

1 cup superfine sugar

1 pound 2 ounces cream cheese

Pinch of salt

3 tablespoons cornstarch

2 eggs, beaten

1 cup sour cream

2 teaspoons vanilla extract

15 ounce can pitted cherries in syrup
   or fruit juice, drained

1. Grease a 9-inch springform pan fitted with a flat bottom. Sift the flour, less 3 tablespoons, with the powdered sugar into a bowl. Rub in 1/2 cup of the butter until the mixture resembles fine breadcrumbs. Add 4 egg yolks, the lemon zest, and heavy whipping cream and mix to form a dough. Shape into a ball, wrap in greaseproof paper, and refrigerate for 20 minutes. Preheat the oven to 375°F.

2. On a lightly floured surface, roll out the dough until it is 1/4 inch thick. Line the bottom and three-quarters of the way up the sides of the prepared pan with the dough. Prick the bottom all over with a fork. Freeze for 10 minutes.

3. When the pastry shell is firm, line it with greaseproof paper and pie weights. Bake blind in the oven for 10–12 minutes, then remove the pie weights and paper and bake for 3–5 minutes. Remove from the oven.

4. In a bowl, rub the remaining flour, butter, and 2 tablespoons of the superfine sugar together to form coarse crumbs, then set aside.

5. Beat the cream cheese in a separate bowl until smooth. Add the salt, cornstarch, and remaining superfine sugar and beat for 1 minute. Gradually add the eggs and remaining egg yolks, beating well to combine. Stir in the sour cream and vanilla extract, mixing well. Fold in the cherries, then spoon the mixture into the pastry shell and smooth the surface.

6. Sprinkle the reserved crumb topping mixture over the top. Bake in the oven for 20 minutes, then reduce the oven temperature to 300°F and bake for a further 30–35 minutes. Turn off the oven and leave the cheesecake inside to cool for 30 minutes. Remove from the oven and set aside to cool completely, then refrigerate before serving.

ICED LIME Traybake

The crunchy topping is just as delicious if you use lemon or orange juice in place of the lime juice. The secret is to pour it over while the cake is still hot so the juice soaks in and the sugar forms a crunchy topping as it cools.

MAKES: 6–8 SQUARES

1 cup/1½ sticks unsalted butter, softened
Generous 1 cup superfine sugar
1⅔ cup self-rising flour
1 teaspoon baking powder
4 large eggs
2 teaspoons finely grated lime zest
10–12 sugar cubes, crushed

FOR THE TOPPING
Thinly pared zest of 2 limes and the juice of 3 limes
½ cup sugar

1. Preheat the oven to 350°F. Lightly grease and line an 11 x 7-inch cake pan or baking pan.

2. For the cake, put all the ingredients except the crushed sugar cubes into a large bowl and beat together until smooth, light and well mixed. Turn the mixture into the prepared pan and smooth the surface. Sprinkle the crushed sugar cubes evenly over the top.

3. Bake in the oven for 40 minutes, or until well risen, golden brown and the top springs back when lightly pressed.

4. Mix the topping ingredients together in a bowl. Remove the cake from the oven and pour the sugar topping evenly over the cake. Leave the cake to cool completely in the pan, then turn out and cut into slices or squares to serve.

SPECIAL OCCASION CAKES

MOTHER'S DAY Cake

A pretty spring cake for Mother's Day, easy enough for kids to make or at least lend a helping hand.

MAKES: 12–16 SLICES

2¼ cups all-purpose flour
1½ cups superfine sugar
¾ cup soft margarine
¾ cup milk
3 eggs, beaten
2½ teaspoons baking powder
1 teaspoon vanilla extract

FOR THE FROSTING
2 lemons
4 cups powdered sugar, sifted
½ cup soft margarine
A few drops of yellow food coloring
Small artificial, fresh, or sugar flowers such as daisies or pansies, to decorate

1. Preheat the oven to 350°F. Grease and flour a 12-inch round pizza pan with a ½-inch-high rim. Grease and flour a 1-quart heat-proof pudding basin.

2. Put all the cake ingredients into a bowl and, using a hand-held electric mixer, beat together until smooth. Spoon just under half of the cake mixture into the prepared basin and level the surface, then spread the rest of the cake mixture in the prepared pizza pan.

3. Place in the oven and bake the pizza pan cake for about 15 minutes and the bowl cake for about 50 minutes, or until risen and golden brown and a skewer inserted into the center of the bowl cake comes out clean. Leave to cool in the pan and basin for 5 minutes, loosen the bowl cake with a round-bladed knife, then turn both cakes onto a wire rack and leave to cool.

4. To make the frosting, finely grate the zest from one of the lemons and squeeze the juice from both. Put the lemon zest and juice into a bowl, add the powdered sugar and margarine and beat together until smooth. Add a few drops of yellow food coloring to give the frosting a pale yellow tint.

5. Place the hat brim (pizza cake) on a cake board. If the top of the bowl cake is rounded, trim it flat with a knife. Attach the flat side of the bowl cake to the center of the pizza cake using a little frosting. Spread the remaining frosting all over the cake using a palette knife, covering the cake completely. Decorate with artificial, fresh, or sugar flowers and serve in slices.

VALENTINE Cake

Don't keep this cake just for Valentine's day—a heart shape is good for an engagement party or even a girl's birthday, just use pink icing, candles, and sparkly ribbon.

MAKES: 16 SLICES

¾ cup soft margarine

2¼ cups unrefined superfine sugar

4 eggs, beaten

1½ cups self-rising flour

4½ tablespoons unsweetened cocoa
   powder, sifted

3½ ounces semi-sweet chocolate,
   melted

FOR THE TOPPING & FROSTING

¾ cup soft margarine

1¾ cups powdered sugar, sifted

4 tablespoons unsweetened cocoa
   powder, sifted

1⅔ pounds poppy-red ready-to-roll
   fondant icing

Sugar roses and ribbon, to decorate

1. Preheat the oven to 350°F. Grease and line a 10 x 10-inch heart-shaped pan.

2. For the cake, beat the margarine and sugar together in a bowl until light and fluffy. Add the eggs, flour, cocoa powder, and melted chocolate and beat together until smooth and well mixed. Spoon the mixture into the prepared pan and smooth the surface.

3. Bake in the oven for 35–40 minutes, or until a skewer inserted into the center comes out clean. Cool in the pan for 5 minutes, then turn out onto a wire rack and leave to cool completely.

4. To make the topping, cream the margarine and one third of the powdered sugar together in a bowl. Gradually beat in the remaining powdered sugar and the cocoa powder, mixing well.

5. Spread the chocolate frosting evenly over the top and sides of the cake. Roll out the red fondant icing and use it to cover the cake. Decorate as desired with sugar roses and ribbon. Serve in slices.

MOLASSES Gingerbread

This rich gingerbread is perfect served at a Halloween party and is delicious served in slices spread with unsalted butter.

MAKES: 8–10 SQUARES

2²/₃ cups all-purpose flour
1 teaspoon baking powder
1 tablespoon ground ginger
1 teaspoon ground cinnamon
1 cup/2 sticks unsalted butter
½ cup molasses
¾ cup light or dark brown sugar
3 eggs, beaten
3 ounces candied cherries, halved
4 ounces pitted dried dates, chopped
2 ounces candied ginger, drained and chopped
¾ cup golden raisins

1. Preheat the oven to 300°F. Grease and line a deep 8-inch square cake pan.

2. Sift the flour, baking powder, ground ginger, and cinnamon into a large bowl. Set aside.

3. Place the butter in a saucepan with the molasses and sugar and stir over a low heat until melted. Pour the melted mixture into the flour mixture and stir to mix well. Beat in the eggs until smooth, then stir in the candied cherries, dates, candied ginger, and golden raisins, mixing well.

4. Pour the mixture evenly into the prepared pan. Bake in the oven for 1–1¼ hours, or until a skewer inserted into the center comes out clean. Cool in the pan for 5 minutes, then turn out onto a wire rack and leave to cool completely. Serve in slices.

CAKE TIP
To measure molasses easily, stand the can in a bowl containing hot water for a few minutes. The molasses will become runny and less sticky,

GREEK EASTER Cake

MAKES: 6-8 SLICES

½ cup/1 stick unsalted butter, softened

½ cup superfine sugar

Finely grated zest of 1 lemon

1 tablespoon lemon juice

2 eggs, beaten

¾ cup semolina

2 teaspoons baking powder

1 cup ground almonds

Greek-style yogurt, to serve (optional)

FOR THE SYRUP

10 cardamom pods

1 orange

1¼ cups superfine sugar

Juice of ½ lemon

2 small cinnamon sticks

1 teaspoon whole cloves

2 tablespoons orange flower water

CAKE TIP
This beautiful sweet-scented cake also makes a lovely summer dessert when served with fresh orange slices.

1. Preheat the oven to 350°F. Grease and line a 8-inch springform cake pan fitted with a flat base.

2. For the cake, cream the butter and sugar together in a bowl until pale and fluffy. Add the lemon zest, lemon juice, eggs, semolina, baking powder, and ground almonds and mix well until smooth. Turn the mixture into the prepared pan and level the surface.

3. Bake in the oven for about 45 minutes, or until just firm to the touch. Leave in the pan for a few minutes, then loosen and turn out onto a wire rack. Remove the lining paper. Clean the pan, then place the very warm cake back into it.

4. While the cake is baking, make the syrup. Lightly crush the cardamom pods. Pare the rind from the orange and cut it into fine strips. Squeeze the juice from the orange and reserve.

5. Put the sugar and scant 1 cup water in a small saucepan and heat gently until the sugar dissolves. Add the lemon juice and boil rapidly for about 3 minutes, or until syrupy. Add the orange strips, orange juice, cardamom, cinnamon sticks, and cloves and cook gently for 5 minutes. Remove the pan from the heat and stir in the orange flower water.

6. Spoon some of the syrup over the very warm cake in the pan. When it has been absorbed, spoon over some more until the cake is steeped in syrup. Set aside to cool in the pan completely, then chill until ready to serve. Remove the cake from the pan and serve in slices (discarding the decorative spices), with syrup from around the cake spooned over. Serve topped with Greek-style yogurt, if you like.

EASTER Cake

MAKES: 12–14 SLICES

3¼ cups luxury mixed dried fruit

2 tablespoons amaretto

¾ cup/1¼ sticks unsalted butter, softened

¾ cup light brown sugar

3 eggs, beaten

Finely grated zest of ½ lemon

1¾ cups self-rising flour

2 teaspoons ground pumpkin pie spice

½ cup ground almonds

16 ounces ready-made natural almond paste or marzipan

8 ounces ready-made yellow almond paste or marzipan

1–2 tablespoons apricot jelly, warmed

Colored ribbon and small chocolate or sugar-coated eggs, to decorate

1. Put the mixed dried fruit in a bowl and sprinkle over the amaretto. Leave to soak for 1 hour. Preheat the oven to 300°F. Grease and line a deep 7-inch round cake pan.

2. Cream the butter and sugar together in a bowl. Beat in the eggs and lemon zest. Fold in the flour, pumpkin pie spice, and ground almonds, then add the dried fruit mixture and mix well. Set aside.

3. Roll out half of the natural almond paste or marzipan on a sheet of non-stick baking paper to form an 7-inch circle. Spoon half of the cake mixture into the base of the prepared pan, spreading it evenly. Place the almond paste circle on top. Spoon over the remaining cake mixture, then level the surface. Bake in the oven for 2–2¼ hours, or until a skewer inserted into the center comes out clean. Turn out onto a wire rack to cool.

4. Roll out the remaining natural almond paste and all but 2 ounces of the yellow paste to form two 7-inch circles and place the yellow one on top of the natural one. Shape 8 balls from the remaining yellow paste.

5. Lightly brush the top of the cake with warm jam, leaving a small circle in the center uncoated. Place the almond circle, yellow-side up, on top of the cake and trim the edges. Using a glass, lightly mark a circle in the centre of the cake. Using a sharp knife, cut through both almond-paste layers up to the edges of the circle to make 8 segments. Lift up the pointed end of each segment and peel it back to reveal the natural almond paste underside. Press it gently into the edge of the cake. Place a yellow almond paste ball on top.

6. Tie a ribbon around the cake and fill the center with sugar-coated chocolate eggs. Serve in slices.

NEW YORK Cheesecake

You can dress up or dress down this Big Apple classic.

Serve it plain or topped with fruit compote.

MAKES: 12–14 SLICES

7 ounces graham crackers, crushed
$\frac{1}{4}$ cup/$\frac{1}{2}$ stick unsalted butter,
   melted
4 x 8-ounce packages cream cheese
Pinch of salt
$1\frac{1}{2}$ cups superfine sugar
1 cup sour cream
2 teaspoons vanilla extract
1 tablespoon finely grated lemon zest
1 tablespoon lemon juice
4 eggs, beaten
2 egg yolks

1. Preheat the oven to 300°F. Grease a 9-inch springform pan fitted with a flat base.

2. In a bowl, mix together the graham cracker crumbs and melted butter, then press this mixture evenly into the base of the prepared pan. Bake in the oven for 10 minutes, or until lightly browned, then remove from the oven and set aside to cool.

3. In a separate bowl, beat the cream cheese until soft and smooth. Add the salt and sugar and beat for 1 minute. Add the sour cream, vanilla extract, lemon zest, and lemon juice and beat for a further 1 minute. Add the eggs and egg yolks and beat until well combined. Pour the mixture evenly over the graham cracker crust in the pan.

4. Bake in the oven for 45–50 minutes, or until the edges are set but the center is still slightly soft. Turn off the oven, leave the cheesecake inside and leave the door ajar. Leave to cool in the oven for 45 minutes.

5. Remove the cheesecake from the oven and cool to room temperature. Remove from the pan, place on a serving plate, cover with foil, and refrigerate for at least 4 hours or preferably overnight, before serving. Serve in slices.

PUMPKIN SPICE Cake

Rich and full-flavored, this dark, spicy cake is great served with fresh cream at a Thanksgiving feast.

MAKES: 15 SLICES

2 cups all-purpose flour
2 teaspoons baking soda
Pinch of salt
3 teaspoons ground cinnamon
1 teaspoon freshly grated nutmeg
1½ teaspoons ground allspice
½ teaspoon ground ginger
1½ cups/2⅔ sticks unsalted butter, softened
1 cup light brown sugar
1 cup superfine sugar
2 eggs, beaten
1 15-ounce can pumpkin purée
2 cups pecans, chopped

1. Preheat the oven to 350°F. Grease, line, and flour a 10-inch Bundt pan.

2. Sift the flour, baking soda, salt, and ground spices into a bowl and set aside. Cream the butter and sugars together in a separate bowl until pale and fluffy, then gradually beat in the eggs.

3. Beat in the pumpkin purée, then stir in the flour mixture and pecans, mixing well. Pour the mixture evenly into the prepared pan.

4. Bake in the oven for 50–60 minutes, or until a skewer inserted into the center comes out clean. Cool in the pan for 10 minutes, then turn out onto a wire rack and leave to cool completely. Serve in slices.

CAKE TIP
For a lighter taste substitute puréed butternut squash for the pumkin.

PANETTONE

MAKES: 8 SLICES

1 tablespoon active dried yeast

2/3 cup warmed milk

3 1/4 cups bread flour

1 egg, beaten

4 egg yolks

2 teaspoons salt

1/4 cup superfine sugar

2 teaspoons finely grated lemon zest

2 teaspoons finely grated orange zest

3/4 cup/1 1/4 sticks unsalted butter, softened

2 1/2 ounces chopped mixed peel

2/3 cup raisins

CAKE TIP

This bread dough takes time to rise. Don't leave it in a very warm place once the butter has been incorporated or it will melt and the dough will be greasy.

1. Grease and line a 6-inch round cake pan with a depth of 4 inches with a double layer of greaseproof paper that is 5 inches higher than the rim of the pan. In a large bowl, dissolve the yeast in 4 tablespoons of the warmed milk. Cover and leave in a warm place for about 10 minutes, or until frothy. Stir in 3/4 cup of the flour and the remaining milk, mixing well. Cover and leave to rise in a warm place for about 30 minutes.

2. In a separate bowl, beat the egg and egg yolks together. Set aside. Sift the remaining flour and salt into the yeast mixture. Make a well in the center and add the sugar, beaten eggs, and lemon and orange zests, mixing to form a soft dough. Knead for about 5 minutes, or until smooth and elastic. Work in the butter until evenly incorporated.

3. Shape the dough into a ball and place in a clean oiled bowl. Cover and leave in a cool place to rise for 2–4 hours, or until doubled in size—the longer the better.

4. Preheat the oven to 400°F. Turn the dough onto a clean surface and knead in the mixed peel and raisins. Shape the dough into a neat ball and place it in the prepared pan. Cut a cross in the top with a sharp knife. Cover and leave to rise again until the dough is 1 inch above the top of the pan.

5. Bake in the oven for 15 minutes, then reduce the oven temperature to 350°F and bake for a further 40 minutes, or until well-risen and golden. Cool in the pan for 10 minutes, then turn out onto a wire rack and leave to cool completely. Serve in slices or wedges.

FESTIVE CHOCOLATE & HAZELNUT Roulade

This special dessert is really easy to make and can even be made the day before the celebration. Decorate with chocolate holly leaves before dusting with extra powdered sugar.

MAKES: 6–8 SLICES

6 eggs, separated
²/₃ cup superfine sugar
2 ounces unsweetened cocoa powder
Sifted powdered sugar, for dusting
Decorations of your choice such as chocolate pieces or holly leaves and holly decorations

FOR THE FILLING
1 cup heavy whipping cream
1 tablespoon brandy
½ cup toasted hazelnuts, finely chopped

1. Preheat the oven to 350°F. Grease and line a 11 x 7-inch jelly roll pan.

2. Whisk the egg yolks in a bowl until they start to thicken. Add the superfine sugar and whisk until the mixture thickens slightly—don't let it get too thick. Sift the cocoa powder over the egg mixture and fold in lightly.

3. In a separate bowl, whisk the egg whites until they form stiff peaks. Using a metal spoon, fold the whisked egg whites into the egg yolk mixture. Pour the mixture evenly into the prepared pan.

4. Bake in the oven for 20–25 minutes, or until risen and springy to the touch. Remove from the oven and leave to cool in the pan. When cold, turn the cake out onto a sheet of greaseproof paper liberally dusted with sifted powdered sugar. Peel off the lining paper.

5. For the filling whip the cream and brandy together in a bowl to form soft peaks, then fold in the hazelnuts. Spread the cream mixture evenly over the roulade. Use the sugar-dusted paper to help you roll up the roulade from one long side.

6. Transfer the roulade to a serving plate while it is still wrapped in the rolling paper. Remove the paper and sift extra powdered sugar over the roulade, if you like. Decorate as desired and serve in slices.

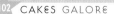

EASY CHRISTENING Cake

MAKES: 10–12 SLICES

6 eggs
½ cup superfine sugar
¾ cup self-rising flour
⅓ cup all-purpose flour

FOR THE FILLING & TOPPING
4 tablespoons strawberry or
    raspberry jelly
5 fluid ounces heavy cream
¼ cup/½ stick unsalted butter,
    softened
1 cup powdered sugar
12 ounces ready-to-roll fondant icing

TO DECORATE
Ribbon (color of your choice)
Decoration of your choice for the
    center of the top of the cake
Pink and/or blue Jordan almonds

CAKE TIP
*To save time, the
sponges can be
frozen, unfilled, for
up to one month.*

1. Preheat the oven to 350°F. Grease, line, and flour the bottom of two 8 inch round cake pans.

2. For the cake, using a hand-held electric mixer, whisk the eggs in a bowl for about 2 minutes. Gradually add the superfine sugar and whisk for a further 5 minutes, or until the mixture is pale, creamy, and thick enough to leave a trail on the surface when the whisk is lifted. Sift the two flours together, then gently fold them into the egg mixture together with 2 tablespoons of hot water. Divide the mixture evenly between the prepared pans and level the surface.

3. Bake in the oven for 20–25 minutes or until golden brown, firm in the center and slightly shrunk away from the sides of the pans. Cool in the pan for 5 minutes, then turn out onto a wire rack and leave to cool completely. When cold, spread one sponge cake with the jelly Whip the cream in a bowl until soft peaks form, then spread the cream over the jam. Place the other sponge cake on top.

4. In a separate bowl, beat the butter and powdered sugar together until pale and fluffy, then spread this evenly over the top and sides of the cake. Using a piece of string, measure up one side, across the top, and down the other side of the cake. Roll out the fondant icing to a circle with a diameter the size you have measured. Carefully lift the fondant icing onto the cake and smooth the top and sides with your hands.

5. For the decoration, tie the ribbon around the cake and place your chosen decoration in the center. Sprinkle the top with Jordan almonds.

VERY EASY CHRISTMAS Cake

This is a very colorful cake, packed full of fruit. You can also use this
mixture to make two or three small cakes to give as gifts.

MAKES: 20 SLICES

1 cup dried apricots, chopped
1 cup red candied cherries
1 cup green candied cherries
1 cup raisins
1 cup mixed candied fruits such as
  pineapple, lemon, ginger, etc.
1/2 cup pitted prunes, halved
1/2 cup Brazil nuts
1/2 cup pecans
1 cup ground almonds
3 eggs
1/4 cup/1/2 stick butter, melted
1/2 cup all-purpose flour
1/2 teaspoon baking powder
3 tablespoons clear honey
2 teaspoons vanilla extract

1. Preheat the oven to 300°F. Grease and line a 11 x 4-inch loaf pan.

2. Put all the fruit, nuts, and ground almonds into a bowl and mix
together well. Set aside.

3. Using a hand-held electric mixer, whisk the eggs in a bowl until the
mixture is pale, creamy, and thick enough to leave a trail on the surface
when the whisk is lifted. Whisk in the melted butter, flour, baking powder,
honey, and vanilla extract until combined, then pour this mixture onto
the fruit mixture and stir to mix well.

4. Turn the mixture into the prepared pan and press down to level the
surface. Bake in the oven for about 1 1/2 hours, or until firm to the touch.
Leave to cool in the pan, then turn out onto a wire rack and leave until
cold. Serve in slices.

CREOLE CHRISTMAS Cake

This is a very rich, moist cake for those who love tradition. The preparation needs to be started a few days before making the cake.

MAKES: 30 SLICES

FOR PRE-SOAKING
5 tablespoons EACH rum, port, brandy, cherry brandy, and water
1 teaspoon Angostura bitters
$\frac{1}{2}$ teaspoon ground cinnamon
$\frac{1}{2}$ teaspoon freshly grated nutmeg
$\frac{1}{2}$ teaspoon ground cloves
$\frac{1}{2}$ teaspoon ground allspice
$\frac{1}{4}$ teaspoon salt
1 teaspoon vanilla extract
1 tablespoon dark brown sugar
6 cups mixed dried fruit

FOR THE CAKE
1 cup/2 sticks unsalted butter, softened
1 cup demerara sugar
4 eggs, beaten
$1\frac{3}{4}$ cups self-rising flour
$\frac{1}{2}$ cup lightly toasted pecans, chopped

TO DECORATE
About 4 tablespoons strained apricot jelly
16 ounces ready-made almond paste or marzipan
16 ounces ready-made icing
Silver balls, etc.

1. Put all the ingredients for pre-soaking into a large saucepan. Bring to a boil and simmer gently for 10 minutes, stirring frequently. Remove the pan from the heat and set aside to cool. Put the cold fruit mixture in an airtight container and leave in the refrigerator for 7 days. Stir the mixture every day.

2. Preheat the oven to 275°F. Grease the bottom and sides of a deep 8-inch square cake pan and double line it with non-stick baking paper.

3. For the cake, cream the butter and sugar together in a bowl. Add the eggs and flour and beat until smooth. Add all of the fruit mixture and the pecans and mix well. Spoon the mixture into the prepared pan and smooth the surface.

4. Cover the pan loosely with a double layer of greaseproof paper and bake in the oven for about $3\frac{1}{2}$ hours, or until just cooked in the center. Remove the cake from the oven and leave to cool completely in the pan, then remove and wrap in greaseproof paper and foil. Leave the wrapped cake in a cool, dry place for a week to allow it to mellow and firm before decorating.

5. To decorate the cake, brush the top and sides with apricot jelly and cover with rolled-out almond paste or marzipan. Spread the royal icing over the top and sides of the cake and swirl decoratively using a palette knife. Add decorations, such as silver balls, as you like. Serve in slices.

CAKES
FOR KIDS

ICED SPONGE Cake

An apricot, golden raisin, and almond topping completes
this delicious, light, and moist sponge cake.

MAKES: 8–10 SLICES

2 cups all-purpose flour
2 teaspoons baking powder
$\frac{1}{2}$ teaspoon salt
$\frac{1}{2}$ cup/1 stick unsalted butter,
  softened
1 cup superfine sugar
3 large eggs, beaten
$1\frac{1}{2}$ teaspoons vanilla extract
$\frac{3}{4}$ cup milk

FOR THE FROSTING
4 egg whites
Pinch of cream of tartar
$\frac{1}{2}$ cup superfine sugar
2 tablespoons chopped dried apricots
2 tablespoons golden raisins
2 tablespoons sliced almonds

1. Preheat the oven to 350°F. Grease and line the bottom of a 9-inch round cake pan.

2. For the cake, sift the flour, baking powder, and salt into a bowl. Set aside. In a separate bowl, cream the butter and sugar together until light and fluffy. Gradually add the eggs, beating well after each addition, then beat in the vanilla extract. Fold in the flour mixture alternately with the milk; mix well.

3. Spoon the mixture into the prepared pan and smooth the surface. Bake in the oven for 30–40 minutes, or until pale golden and a skewer inserted into the center comes out clean. Cool in the pan for 5 minutes, then turn out onto a wire rack and leave to cool completely.

4. To make the frosting, using a hand-held electric mixer, whisk the egg whites and cream of tartar together in a bowl until stiff, then gradually whisk in the sugar, until the mixture is stiff and glossy.

5. Place the cake on an ovenproof serving plate. Swirl the frosting evenly over the top of the cake, then sprinkle the top with the apricots, golden raisins, and almonds. Return the cake to a warm oven for 4–5 minutes to give the frosting a little color. Remove from the oven and set aside to cool. Serve in slices and eat on day of making.

BAKED ALASKA BIRTHDAY Cake

Dim the lights and light the candles. This is an all-time favorite celebration cake and the fresh raspberries make it extra special.

MAKES: 6–8 SLICES

³/₄ cup/1¹/₂ sticks unsalted butter, softened

³/₄ cup sugar

3 eggs, beaten

1 teaspoon vanilla extract

1¹/₂ cups self-rising flour, sifted

12 ounces raspberry jelly

1¹/₂ cups fresh raspberries

4 egg whites

1 cup superfine sugar

8 scoops of vanilla or your favorite ice cream

Candles or sparklers, to decorate (optional)

1. Preheat the oven to 350°F. Grease and line the bottom of a deep 8-inch round cake pan.

2. Cream the butter and sugar together in a large bowl until pale and fluffy. Gradually add the eggs, beating well after each addition, then beat in the vanilla extract. Fold in the flour, mixing well.

3. Spoon the mixture into the prepared pan and smooth the surface. Bake in the oven for 30–35 minutes, or until risen and golden. Turn out onto a wire rack and leave to cool.

4. Increase the oven temperature to 425°F. Cut the sponge cake in half horizontally. Place the base sponge round on a baking sheet and spread with the jelly. Place the second sponge round on top. Arrange the raspberries on top of the sponge cake.

5. Whisk the egg whites in a large bowl until they form stiff peaks. Slowly whisk in the superfine sugar to make a thick, glossy meringue mixture.

6. Place scoops of ice cream over the raspberries to cover. Spread the meringue mixture evenly over the ice cream and sides of the sponge so that everything is covered. Bake in the oven for 8–10 minutes. Remove from the oven, decorate with birthday candles or sparklers, if using, and serve immediately in slices.

CHOCOLATE PEANUT BUTTER Cake

MAKES: 20 SLICES

1 cup/2 sticks unsalted butter, softened
2 cups light brown sugar
$^1/_2$ cup chunky peanut butter
4 ounces semi-sweet chocolate, melted
1$^3/_4$ cups all-purpose flour
2 teaspoons baking powder
$^1/_2$ teaspoon baking soda
4 eggs, beaten
5 tablespoons milk

FOR THE GLAZE & DECORATION
2 tablespoons butter
2 tablespoons smooth peanut butter
3 tablespoons light corn syrup
1 teaspoon vanilla extract
1 cup semi-sweet chocolate chips
$^1/_4$ cup powdered sugar
5 ounces semi-sweet chocolate, broken into squares
Chocolate-coated peanuts (optional)

1. Preheat the oven to 350°F. Grease and line the bottom of a flat-bottomed 10-inch round cake pan.

2. For the cake, beat the butter and sugar together in a bowl until light and fluffy. Beat in the peanut butter and melted chocolate. Sift the flour, baking powder, and baking soda into a separate bowl. Beat the eggs into the creamed mixture a little at a time, adding a little flour if the mixture shows any sign of curdling. Fold in the remaining flour and milk, mixing well. Turn the mixture into the prepared pan and smooth the surface.

3. Bake in the oven for about 50 minutes, or until a skewer inserted into the center comes out clean. Cool in the pan for a few minutes, then turn out onto a wire rack and leave to cool completely.

4. To make the glaze, put the butter, peanut butter, light corn syrup, and vanilla extract into a saucepan. Heat gently until the butter has melted, stirring. Add the chocolate chips and stir until completely melted and smooth. Stir in the icing sugar. Remove the pan from the heat and leave to cool until it is of a thick pouring consistency.

5. Meanwhile, melt the plain chocolate and spread it evenly on a baking sheet lined with non-stick baking paper. Chill until almost set. Using a small star-shaped cookie cutter, stamp out stars in the set chocolate. Leave until completely set and then lift them off the paper.

6. Pour the glaze evenly over the cake and decorate with chocolate stars and chocolate-coated peanuts, if using. Serve in slices.

ROCKY ROAD Cake

Mini marshmallows, walnuts, and chocolate caramels make

a rich icing for this all-time favorite cake.

MAKES: 8–10 SLICES

1½ cups self-rising flour

2 teaspoons baking powder

4 tablespoons unsweetened cocoa
   powder

Pinch of salt

1 cup/2 sticks unsalted butter,
   softened

1¼ cups superfine sugar

4 eggs, beaten

6 tablespoons buttermilk

2 teaspoons vanilla extract

FOR THE FILLING & TOPPING

35 chocolate-covered caramels

3 tablespoons milk

2 cups mini marshmallows

1 cup walnuts, chopped

CAKE TIP

*Top the iced cake with
any decorations of your
choice, such as chopped
chocolate-covered caramels,
milk chocolate buttons,
marshmallows, and/or
hazelnuts and pecans.*

1. Preheat the oven to 350°F. Grease and line the bottom of two 8-inch round cake pans.

2. For the cake, sift the flour, baking powder, cocoa powder and salt into a bowl. In a separate bowl, beat the butter until pale and fluffy. Add the sugar and beat for a further 2 minutes. Gradually add the eggs, beating well after each addition, then stir in the buttermilk and vanilla extract.

3. Stir in the dry ingredients, mixing well. Spoon the mixture into the prepared pans, dividing it evenly, and smooth the surface. Bake in the oven for 30–35 minutes, or until firm to the touch. Turn the cakes out onto a wire rack and leave to cool.

4. Cut small slits into the top of each sponge cake and set aside. For the filling and topping, put the chocolate caramels in a saucepan with the milk and ½ cup of the marshmallows and heat gently until melted, stirring. Put one sponge cake on a plate and pour over half of the melted chocolate mixture. Sprinkle over half of the walnuts.

5. Place the second sponge cake on top and pour over the remaining chocolate mixture. Sprinkle with the remaining marshmallows and walnuts. Serve in slices.

MARBLE Cheesecake

This is a great cheesecake to serve for kids with its attractive swirl of chocolate—who could resist.

MAKES: 12–14 SLICES

7 ounces graham cracker crumbs
4 tablespoons unsalted butter, melted
3 (8-ounce) packages cream cheese
Pinch salt
3 tablespoons cornstarch
Scant 1 cup sugar
2 eggs
2 egg yolks
2 teaspoons vanilla extract
2 cups heavy cream
5 ounces dark chocolate, melted
4 tablespoons unsweetened cocoa powder
2 teaspoons vanilla seeds

1. Preheat the oven to 150°C. Grease a 9-inch springform pan.

2. Mix together the graham cracker crumbs and melted butter, and press into the bottom of the prepared pan. Bake for 10 minutes, or until lightly browned, then leave to cool.

3. Beat the cheese until smooth. Add the salt, cornstarch, and sugar, and beat for 1 minute. Gradually add the eggs, beating to combine. Stir in the vanilla. Whip the cream, and fold into the mixture. Divide the mixture equally between two bowls. Add the melted chocolate and cocoa to one and mix well. Stir the vanilla seeds into the other bowl.

4. Spoon half the chocolate mixture into the pan then spoon the vanilla mix over the top. Spoon over the remaining chocolate mix and draw a knife through the mix to create a swirled marble effect.

5. Bake for 55–60 minutes, or until set at the edge but slightly soft in the center. Turn off the oven and cool in the oven for 45 minutes.

6. Remove the cheesecake from the oven and cool to room temperature. Remove from the pan, cover with foil, and refrigerate until cold.

COCONUT CREAM Cake

A tasty classic—add to the kids' lunch boxes or indulge yourself.

MAKES: 8–10 SLICES

¾ cup/1¼ sticks unsalted butter, softened
¾ cup superfine sugar
1 cup buttermilk
1 teaspoon vanilla extract
1⅓ cups all-purpose flour
1 teaspoon baking powder
½ teaspoon baking soda
Pinch of salt
1 cup flaked or shredded coconut
4 egg whites

CAKE TIP
To revive dry coconut flakes, cover with milk and refrigerate for a couple of hours. Drain and pat dry before using.

1. Preheat the oven to 350°F. Grease and line the bottom of a deep 9-inch round cake pan.

2. Cream the butter and sugar together in a bowl until pale and fluffy, then mix in the buttermilk and vanilla extract. Sift the flour, baking powder, baking soda and salt into the bowl and fold in until combined. Add the coconut, less 2 tablespoons, and mix well.

3. In a separate bowl, whisk the egg whites until stiff. Stir one third of the whisked egg whites into the cake mixture to loosen it, then fold in the remainder. Pour the mixture evenly into the prepared pan and sprinkle with the reserved 2 tablespoons of coconut.

4. Bake in the oven for 30–35 minutes, or until golden and firm to the touch. Turn out onto a wire rack and leave to cool. Serve in slices.

PINK & WHITE Cake

MAKES: 16 SLICES

FOR THE PLAIN CAKE
³/₄ cup vegetable margarine
³/₄ cup superfine sugar
3 eggs, beaten
1¹/₄ cups self-rising flour

FOR THE PINK CAKE
³/₄ cups vegetable margarine
³/₄ cup superfine sugar
3 eggs, beaten
1¹/₄ cups self-rising flour
Pink food coloring

FOR THE FROSTING & DECORATION
2 cups soft margarine
8 cups powdered sugar, sifted
Pink food coloring
Cake candles, to decorate

1. Preheat the oven to 350°F. To make the plain cake, grease and line the bottom of two 8-inch round cake pans.

2. Beat the fat and sugar together in a bowl until light and creamy. Add the eggs and flour and beat until smooth. Divide the mixture evenly between the prepared pans and level the surface. Bake in the oven for 20–25 minutes, or until risen and firm to the touch. Cool in the pans for a few minutes, then turn out onto a wire rack and leave to cool completely.

3. To make the pink cakes, follow the same method as for the plain cakes but add some pink food coloring to the fat and sugar mixture, mixing well. Bake and cool the cakes as above.

4. To make the frosting, put the margarine into a bowl and gradually beat in the powdered sugar. Add some pink food colouring, mixing well.

5. To assemble the cakes, place them on a large work surface. Using a 4¹/₂-inch and a 2-inch plain round cookie cutter, cut rings from each cake. Carefully lift the central ring from each cake and replace it with one of the other color. Spread a little frosting over each cake and stack them on top of one another, making sure you alternate the cakes to give a checkerboard effect.

6. Spread a little of the frosting over the top of the cake. Using a piping bag fitted with a star tip, pipe lines of frosting down the sides of the cake and around the top edge. Arrange candles on top of the cake in the center and pipe the remaining frosting decoratively in a circle around them. Serve in slices.

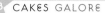

MARSHMALLOW JELLY Surprise

With marshmallows on top and a surprise layer of jelly inside, this cake is great to make when friends come to visit.

MAKES: 8–10 SLICES

¹/₂ cup soft margarine
¹/₂ cup superfine sugar
1 cup self-rising flour
2 eggs, beaten
2–3 tablespoons black cherry jelly or any red jelly of your choice
1 cup large white or pink marshmallows
1¹/₄ cups powdered sugar

1. Preheat the oven to 350°F. Grease and line the bottom of a deep 7-inch round cake pan. Put the margarine, sugar, flour, and eggs into a bowl and beat together until smooth and well mixed.

2. Spread half of the mixture into the bottom of the prepared pan. Dot with the jelly. Spread the remaining cake mixture evenly over the top. Bake in the oven for about 40–45 minutes, or until well risen and golden brown.

3. While the cake is cooking, cut the marshmallows in half horizontally, using wetted scissors. Remove the cake from the oven and leave to cool in the pan for a few minutes, then turn out onto a wire rack. Cool the cake for about 15 minutes, then arrange the marshmallows, cut-side down, over the top of the warm cake (the cake needs to be warm enough for the cut sides of the marshmallows to melt slightly so that they stick to the cake). Leave the cake until quite cold.

4. Mix together the powdered sugar and enough water in a bowl to make a thick pouring consistency. Pour the icing over the cake and allow it to run slightly down the sides. Serve in slices.

CHOCOLATE RIPPLE Cake

Serve this cake thickly sliced to reveal the luscious chocolate ripples.

MAKES: 12–14 SLICES

7 ounces semi-sweet chocolate, broken into squares

1¼ cups/2 sticks unsalted butter, softened

2 tablespoons light brown sugar

½ teaspoon ground cinnamon

1 cup superfine sugar

3 eggs, beaten

2 teaspoons vanilla extract

1½ cups self-rising flour

½ teaspoon baking powder

3½ ounces milk chocolate chunks

CAKE TIP
When melting chocolate remember that the smaller the pieces the quicker and more evenly the chocolate will melt.

1. Preheat the oven to 350°F. Grease and line the bottom of a 10-inch loaf pan. Melt the milk chocolate with 3 tablespoons of the butter in a heat-proof bowl set over a pan of simmering water. Remove the bowl from the heat and stir in the brown sugar and cinnamon. Set aside.

2. Beat the remaining butter and superfine sugar together in a bowl until pale and fluffy. Add the eggs and vanilla extract, then sift the flour and baking powder into the bowl. Beat together until smooth and well mixed.

3. Spread one-quarter of the mixture into the bottom of the prepared pan. Spread one-third of the melted chocolate mixture over the cake mixture. Repeat the layering twice more, then finish with a layer of cake mixture spread evenly on top.

4. Sprinkle the chocolate chunks evenly over the top. Bake in the oven for about 45–60 minutes, or until a skewer inserted into the center comes out clean. Cool in the pan for 5–10 minutes, then turn out onto a wire rack and leave to cool completely. Serve in slices.

CHOCO-MALT Cake

A great favorite for big and little kids, this cake goes well with a glass of milk, and with the addition of a few birthday candles, it makes a great party cake.

MAKES: **10–12 SLICES**

Scant 1 cup soft margarine or
    softened butter
Generous 1 cup superfine sugar
3/4 cup instant malted milk powder
1/3 cup unsweetened cocoa powder,
    sifted
4 eggs, beaten
1 1/2 cups self-rising flour, sifted
4 tablespoons milk

FOR THE FROSTING & DECORATION
4 tablespoons boiling water
1/3 cup instant malted milk powder
2 tablespoons unsweetened cocoa
    powder
1/2 cup soft margarine or softened
    butter
2 cups powdered sugar, sifted
Chocolate-coated malted milk balls,
    such as Maltesers, to decorate

1. Preheat the oven to 350°F. Grease and line the bottom of two 8-inch round cake pans.

2. For the cake, cream the margarine or butter and sugar together in a bowl until blended. Add the malted milk powder, cocoa powder, eggs, flour and milk and beat together until smooth and creamy. Divide the mixture evenly between the prepared pans and smooth the surface.

3. Bake in the oven for about 30 minutes, or until well risen and firm to the touch. Cool in the pan for a few minutes, then turn out onto a wire rack and leave to cool completely.

4. To make the frosting, blend the boiling water, malted milk powder, and cocoa powder together in a bowl, then set aside to cool.

5. In a separate bowl, beat the margarine and half of the powdered sugar together until creamy, then add the remaining powdered sugar and the blended cocoa mixture, mixing well. Sandwich the two cakes together with half of the frosting, then spread the remaining frosting over the top. Scatter the chocolate-coated malted milk balls on top. Serve in slices.

JELLY BEAN Roll

This homemade sponge cake filled with your favorite jelly is quick and easy to make—ideal for children's parties.

MAKES: 6–8 SLICES

²/₃ cup self-rising flour
1½ teaspoons baking powder
Pinch of salt
3 eggs
¾ cup superfine sugar, plus
   2 tablespoons
½ teaspoon vanilla extract
2 tablespoons lowfat milk
6 tablespoons strawberry jelly
3 tablespoons unsalted butter, softened
1 cup powdered sugar, sifted
Jelly beans, to decorate

CAKE TIP
Instead of jelly, try lemon or orange curd, chocolate spread, or even marshmallow cream.

1. Preheat the oven to 375°F. Grease and line a 9 x 11-inch jelly roll pan.

2. Sift the flour, baking powder, and salt into a bowl and set aside. Using a hand-held electric mixer, whisk the eggs and ¾ cup of the superfine sugar together in a large bowl until the mixture is pale, creamy, and thick enough to leave a trail on the surface when the whisk is lifted. Stir in the vanilla extract and milk.

3. Gently fold the dry ingredients into the egg mixture, then pour the mixture evenly into the prepared pan. Bake in the oven for 8–10 minutes, or until just firm to the touch.

4. Sprinkle a sheet of greaseproof paper with the remaining 2 tablespoons of superfine sugar and turn the sponge out onto it. Peel away the lining paper, then roll up the sponge from a long side, with the greaseproof paper inside. Transfer to a wire rack and leave to cool for 10–15 minutes.

5. Unroll the sponge cake and discard the greaseproof paper, then spread the sponge evenly with strawberry jelly and re-roll tightly. Beat the butter in a bowl until pale and fluffy, then beat in the powdered sugar, mixing well. Using a piping bag fitted with a plain tip, pipe the butter icing over the cake and decorate with jelly beans.

ICED RASPBERRY Cake

For this simple and quick dessert, frozen raspberries are used straight from the freezer. Chill the cake well before serving.

MAKES: 8–10 SLICES

5 tablespoons/²/₃ stick unsalted butter, melted

2 cups crushed graham crackers

¼ cup light brown sugar

6 ounces raspberry jelly

3 cups frozen raspberries

20 large pink marshmallows

4 tablespoons milk

2 cups heavy cream

CAKE TIP
An easy way to cut up jelly is to use wet kitchen scissors.

1. Preheat the oven to 350°F. Mix the melted butter, graham cracker crumbs, and sugar in a bowl, then press this mixture evenly into the bottom of a 9-inch springform pan fitted with a flat base. Bake in the oven for 10 minutes, then remove from the oven and set aside to cool.

2. Dissolve the raspberry jelly in ½ cup boiling water in a heat-proof measuring cup or bowl, then stir in the frozen raspberries. Pour this mixture evenly over the prepared case in the pan. Set aside until the jelly is cool and set.

3. Place the marshmallows and milk in a saucepan and heat gently until melted, stirring. Pour into a heat-proof bowl and set aside to cool.

4. Whip the cream lightly in a separate bowl, then fold it through the cooled marshmallow mixture. Spoon the marshmallow cream on top of the raspberry jelly in the pan, spreading it evenly. Refrigerate for 2–3 hours before serving. Serve in slices.

CHOCOLATE CHIP & VANILLA Cake

For a simple sheet cake use an oblong cake pan, but for something fancier try using a 7½ x 4-inch Angel food cake pan.

MAKES: 12–16 SLICES

1 cup soft margarine
1 cup superfine sugar
1¾ cups self-rising flour
4 eggs, beaten
2 tablespoons milk
2 tablespoons unsweetened cocoa powder
2 tablespoons hot water
1 teaspoon vanilla extract
½ cup semi-sweet chocolate chips
½ cup white chocolate chips

1. Preheat the oven to 350°F. Grease and line the bottom of a 11 x 7-inch cake pan.

2. Put the margarine, sugar, flour, eggs, and milk into a bowl and beat together until smooth and well mixed. Spoon half of the mixture into a separate bowl. Mix the cocoa powder with the hot water in a small bowl and leave to cool slightly.

3. Mix the vanilla extract and ¼ cup of the semi-sweet chocolate chips into one of the bowls of cake mixture. Place spoonfuls of this mixture randomly in the prepared pan.

4. Mix the blended cocoa and ¼ cup of the white chocolate chips into the cake mixture in the second bowl. Spoon the chocolate mixture in between the plain mixture in the pan to fill in the gaps. Drag the handle of a teaspoon through the mixtures to create a marbled effect.

5. Bake in the oven for about 30 minutes, or until firm to the touch. Remove the cake from the oven and leave it to cool completely in the pan. Turn out the cake and place it on a serving plate. Melt the remaining semi-sweet and white chocolate chips separately, then drizzle them decoratively over the top of the cake. Serve in slices.

HEDGEHOG Cake

Deceptively easy to make, this charming cake is ideal for a
small child's birthday party.

MAKES: **12–18 SLICES**

1½ cups self-rising flour
1 cup superfine sugar
½ cup/1 stick unsalted butter,
   softened
2 eggs, beaten
2 tablespoons drinking chocolate
   powder
5 tablespoons evaporated milk
5 tablespoons water

FOR THE FROSTING & DECORATION

½ cup/1 stick unsalted butter,
   softened
2 cups powdered sugar, sifted
2 tablespoons evaporated milk
4 ounces ready-made almond paste
   or marzipan, tinted brown with
   food coloring
10–12 chocolate flake bars
1 red sugar-coated hard candy
2 semi-sweet or milk chocolate chips

1. Preheat the oven to 350°F. Grease and line the bottom of a 1-quart ovenproof round-bottomed glass pudding basin. Put all the cake ingredients into a bowl and beat together well until light and fluffy. Spoon the mixture into the prepared basin and smooth the surface, then place the basin on a baking sheet.

2. Bake in the oven for about 1 hour, or until a skewer inserted into the center comes out clean. Cool in the basin for 5–10 minutes, loosen around the edges of the cake with a round-bladed knife, then turn out onto a wire rack and leave to cool completely.

3. To make the frosting, beat the butter, powdered sugar, and evaporated milk together in a bowl. Trim the top of the cake so it is flat, then place it cut-side down and cut it in half vertically. Spread a little frosting over the cut sides of each half of the cake and join back together to make the semi-circular hedgehog body.

4. Place the cake on a cake board. Mold the almond paste into a small cone shape for the head and attach it to the body with a little frosting. Spread the remaining frosting all over the body, covering it completely. Cut the chocolate flakes into small 2-inch lengths and push them into the frosting at a slight angle, to create the hedgehog spikes. Attach the red candy on the tip of the head for a nose and the chocolate chips for the eyes. Serve in slices.

PEPPERMINT-CHOCOLATE LAYER Cake

Crunchy peppermints top this minty, frosted chocolate cake—a sure-fire favorite with kids.

MAKES: 10–12 SLICES

7 ounces dark bitter chocolate,
   broken into squares
5 tablespoons unsalted butter
2$\frac{1}{2}$ cups superfine sugar
3 egg yolks
1$\frac{1}{2}$ cups milk
2 cups self-rising flour
Pinch of salt
$\frac{1}{4}$ teaspoon baking soda
2 teaspoons vanilla extract

FOR THE FROSTING
3 egg whites
2 cups superfine sugar
Pinch of salt
$\frac{1}{4}$ teaspoon cream of tartar
2–3 drops of green food coloring
2–3 drops of peppermint extract
$\frac{1}{4}$ cup crushed peppermint candies

1. Preheat the oven to 350°F. Grease and line the bottom of two 8-inch round cake pans.

2. For the cake, melt the chocolate and butter in a large heat-proof bowl set over a pan of gently simmering water. Remove from the heat and leave to cool to room temperature. Stir in the sugar, then add the egg yolks and half of the milk and stir to mix well.

3. Add the flour, salt and baking soda and beat for 1 minute using a hand-held electric mixer. Beat in the remaining milk and the vanilla extract. Spoon the mixture into the prepared pans, dividing it evenly, and level the surface.

4. Bake in the oven for 25–30 minutes, or until just firm to the touch. Turn out onto a wire rack and leave to cool.

5. To make the frosting, mix the egg whites, sugar, salt, cream of tartar, and 3 tablespoons of water in a heat-proof bowl set over a pan of gently simmering water. Whisk for about 7 minutes, or until the mixture forms firm peaks. Remove the bowl from the heat and stir in the food colouring and peppermint extract. Sandwich the two cakes together with some frosting, then spread the remaining frosting evenly over the top and sides of the cake. Decorate with the crushed sweets.

DESSERT
CAKES

WALNUT & STRAWBERRY Cake

MAKES: 8–10 SLICES

1/3 cup walnuts
4 eggs
Scant 1 cup superfine sugar
1/2 cup all-purpose flour, sifted
1 teaspoon baking powder

FOR THE FROSTING & DECORATION
1 egg white
3/4 cup superfine sugar
A few drops of rose water
7 ounces small strawberries, hulled
1/3 cup walnuts, finely chopped, to
    decorate

1. Preheat the oven to 350°F. Grease and line a 8-inch springform pan fitted with a flat base.

2. Process the walnuts in a blender or food processor until finely chopped—don't over-process or the nuts will become oily. Set aside.

3. Using a hand-held electric mixer, whisk the eggs and sugar together in a large heat-proof bowl set over a pan of simmering water, until pale, creamy and thick enough to leave a trail. Remove from the heat.

4. Sift the flour and baking powder over the egg mixture and fold in gently together with the processed walnuts until well mixed. Pour the mixture evenly into the prepared pan. Bake in the oven for 40–45 minutes, or until well risen, golden, and just firm to the touch. Cool in the pan for 5 minutes, then turn out onto a wire rack and leave to cool completely.

5. To make the frosting, put the egg white, sugar, 1 tablespoon of water, and the rose water in a heat-proof bowl set over a pan of simmering water. Using a hand-held electric mixer, whisk the ingredients together for about 10–12 minutes, or until thick. Remove from the heat.

6. Up to 4 hours before serving, slice the cake in half horizontally. Sandwich the two cake halves together with a little frosting and some sliced strawberries, reserving a few strawberries to decorate.

7. Spread the remaining frosting over the top and sides of the cake. Halve the rest of the strawberries and arrange them on top of the cake. Press the chopped walnuts over the sides of the cake. Serve in slices.

SUMMER FRUIT Roulade

A light sponge cake encases sumptuous summer fruits and kirsch-flavored whipped cream.

MAKES: 6–8 SLICES

5 large eggs, separated

Generous ½ cup superfine sugar

3 ounces creamed coconut (in a
   block), grated

8 ounces frozen mixed summer fruits

1 tablespoon freshly squeezed
   orange juice

2 teaspoons cornstarch

½ cup heavy whipping cream

2 teaspoons Kirsch

Sifted powdered sugar, for dusting

2 tablespoons flaked or shredded
   coconut

1. Preheat the oven to 350°F. Grease and line a 11 x 13-inch jelly roll pan.

2. Whisk the egg yolks and superfine sugar together in a bowl until thick and glossy. In a separate bowl, whisk the egg whites until they form stiff peaks. Fold the creamed coconut into the egg yolk mixture. Gently stir in half of the whisked egg whites, then fold in the rest. Pour the mixture evenly into the prepared pan.

3. Bake in the oven for about 20 minutes, or until risen and firm to the touch. Remove from the oven and leave to cool in the pan, covered with a wire rack and a clean damp dish towel.

4. Cook the summer fruits in a saucepan with the orange juice until the juices begin to run. Blend the cornstarch with a little water and stir into the fruit. Cook until thickened, stirring, then remove the pan from the heat and set aside to cool. Whip the cream and kirsch together in a bowl to form soft peaks.

5. Liberally dust a piece of greaseproof paper with sifted powdered sugar, then turn the sponge cake out onto it. Peel off the lining paper. Spread the cake evenly with the whipped cream and then the fruit.

6. Using the paper underneath to help, roll up the roulade from one long side. Transfer to a serving plate while it is still wrapped in the rolling paper. Remove the paper and sprinkle the roulade with flaked or shredded coconut. Sift powdered sugar on top. Serve in slices.

GOOEY CHOCOLATE Cake

Sheer, outrageous indulgence—this cake is deliciously gooey and melts in the mouth. It is utterly irresistible whatever the occasion!

MAKES: 8–10 SLICES

11 ounces dark bitter chocolate (at least 70% cocoa solids), broken into squares
3/4 cup/1 1/4 sticks unsalted butter
8 eggs, separated
1 cup light brown sugar
1/2 cup ground almonds

FOR THE TOPPING & DECORATION
4 1/2 ounces semi-sweet chocolate, melted
4 1/2 ounces milk chocolate, melted
Chocolate-dipped fresh strawberries, to decorate

1. Preheat the oven to 350°F. Grease a 8-inch springform pan fitted with a flat base, then line the bottom and sides of the pan with foil.

2. For the cake, melt the chocolate and butter in a large, heat-proof bowl set over a pan of simmering water. Remove from heat and leave to cool.

3. In a separate bowl, whisk the egg yolks and sugar together until thick and pale. Stir in the cooled chocolate and butter mixture, then stir in the ground almonds.

4. In another bowl, whisk the egg whites until stiff, then fold them into the chocolate mixture. Pour the mixture evenly into the prepared pan. Place the pan in a roasting pan half full of boiling water.

5. Place in the oven and bake for 1–1 1/4 hours, or until the cake is quite firm, yet a skewer inserted into the center comes out a little sticky. Remove the cake from the oven and leave to cool completely in the pan, then turn it out and place on a serving plate.

6. For the topping, drizzle the melted semi-sweet and milk chocolates decoratively over the cake. Decorate with chocolate-dipped strawberries and serve in slices.

HAZELNUT MERINGUE Cake

This rich yet light hazelnut meringue filled with bourbon-laced cream and fresh raspberries makes an impressive dinner party dessert. Fill the meringue about 1 hour before serving—any longer and it will start to get soft.

MAKES: 8–10 SLICES

4 egg whites
Scant 1 cup superfine sugar
1 teaspoon vanilla extract
1 teaspoon cider vinegar
1 teaspoon cornstarch
²⁄₃ cup toasted hazelnuts, finely ground
2 tablespoons coarsely chopped toasted hazelnuts

FOR THE FILLING
²⁄₃ cup natural yogurt
2 tablespoons bourbon
2 tablespoons clear honey
¹⁄₂ cup heavy whipping cream
8 ounces fresh raspberries
Sifted powdered sugar, for dusting

1. Preheat the oven to 350°F. Grease and line two 8-inch round cake pans.

2. For the meringue, whisk the egg whites in a bowl until they form stiff peaks. Gradually whisk in the sugar to make a stiff and glossy meringue. Fold in the vanilla extract, vinegar, cornstarch, and ground hazelnuts.

3. Divide the mixture evenly between the two prepared pans and level the surface. Scatter the chopped hazelnuts over the top of one, then bake in the oven for 50–60 minutes, or until crisp. Turn out onto a wire rack and leave to cool.

4. For the filling, stir the yogurt, bourbon, and honey together in a bowl. In a separate bowl, whip the cream until it forms soft peaks, then fold into the yogurt mixture together with the raspberries.

5. Sandwich the two meringues together with the cream mixture, with the nut-topped meringue uppermost. Dust with sifted powdered sugar. Serve in slices.

CHOCOLATE & RASPBERRY Torte

MAKES: 10–12 SLICES

½ cup all-purpose flour
4 tablespoons unsweetened cocoa
  powder, plus extra for dusting
3 large eggs
¼ cup superfine sugar
5 tablespoons unsalted butter,
  melted

FOR THE FILLING
14 fluid ounces heavy cream
4 tablespoons orange-flavored liqueur
1½ cups fresh or frozen and thawed
  raspberries
1 tablespoon powdered sugar
2 ounces semi-sweet chocolate,
  grated

1. Preheat the oven to 350°F. Grease and line a deep 9-inch round cake pan. Sift the flour and cocoa powder into a bowl.

2. Using a hand-held electric mixer, whisk the eggs and superfine sugar together in a large heat-proof bowl set over a pan of simmering water, until the mixture is pale, creamy, and thick enough to leave a trail on the surface when the whisk is lifted. Remove from the heat.

3. In three batches, sift the flour and cocoa powder over the whisked egg mixture and gently fold in, drizzling a little melted butter around the edge of the bowl between each batch.

4. Pour the mixture evenly into the prepared pan. Bake in the oven for about 20 minutes, or until golden brown and the top springs back when lightly pressed. Cool in the pan for 2–3 minutes, then turn out onto a wire rack and leave to cool completely.

5. Whip the cream and liqueur together in a bowl to form soft peaks. Fold in the raspberries, powdered sugar, and chocolate.

6. Slice the cake in half horizontally. Grease and line a an 8-inch springform pan fitted with a flat base and trim the cake to fit the base of the pan. Put one of the cake halves at the bottom of the pan. Pile in the raspberry cream, spreading it evenly, then top with the remaining cake half. Press down evenly and freeze for about 4 hours, or until the filling is firm.

7. Dust the top of the cake with sifted cocoa powder, then remove from the pan and serve in slices.

WHITE CHOCOLATE AMARETTO Cheesecake

MAKES: 10–12 SLICES

16–18 graham crackers

3–4 amaretti cookies

1/4 cup/1/2 stick unsalted butter, melted

1/2 teaspoon almond extract

1/2 teaspoon ground cinnamon

FOR THE FILLING

12 ounces good-quality white chocolate, broken into squares

1/2 cup heavy whipping cream

3 x 8-ounce packages cream cheese, softened

1/3 cup superfine sugar

4 eggs

2 tablespoons Amaretto liqueur or 1/2 teaspoon almond extract

1/2 teaspoon vanilla extract

FOR THE TOPPING

1 3/4 cups sour cream

1/4 cup superfine sugar

1 tablespoon Amaretto or 1/2 teaspoon almond extract

White chocolate curls, to decorate

1. Preheat the oven to 350°F. Grease a 9-inch springform pan fitted with a flat base. Put the crackers in a blender or food processor and pulse into fine crumbs. Add the butter, almond extract, and cinnamon and blend to mix. Press the mixture into the bottom and sides of the prepared pan.

2. Bake in the oven for 5 minutes, then remove from the oven and transfer to a wire rack to cool. Reduce the temperature to 300°F.

3. For the filling, melt the chocolate and cream together in a saucepan over a low heat, stirring until smooth. Remove from the heat and set aside. Beat the cream cheese in a bowl until smooth. Gradually add the sugar, then each egg, beating well after each addition. Slowly beat in the melted chocolate mixture, Amaretto or almond extract, and vanilla extract.

4. Spoon the mixture evenly over the crust in the pan. Place the pan on a baking sheet and bake in the oven for 45–55 minutes, or until the edge of the cheesecake is firm, but the center is slightly soft. Transfer to a wire rack. Increase the oven temperature to 400°F.

5. For the topping, beat the sour cream, sugar, and Amaretto or almond extract together in a bowl. Spread evenly over the cheesecake and bake for 5–7 minutes. Turn off the oven, but leave the cheesecake inside for 1 hour, then transfer to a wire rack to cool. Run a sharp knife around the edge of the cheesecake, but leave in the pan. Refrigerate, loosely covered, overnight.

6. To serve, unclip and remove the cheesecake from the pan. Transfer to a serving plate and decorate with white chocolate curls. Serve in slices.

BLUEBERRY & WHITE CHOCOLATE
Meringue Roll

This is rather an unusual idea, using a meringue mixture to roll into a roulade-type dessert. The filling is a white chocolate cream with tangy, fragrant blueberries throughout.

MAKES: 10–12 SLICES

²/₃ cup superfine sugar

Seeds from ¹/₂ vanilla bean

5 egg whites

Sifted powdered sugar, for dusting

5 ounces white chocolate, broken into squares

¹/₂ cup natural yogurt

2¹/₂ cups mascarpone cheese

²/₃ cup fresh blueberries

CAKE TIP
For a lighter dessert use low fat soft cheese instead of mascarpone.

1. Preheat the oven to 425°F. Grease and line an 11 x 13-inch jelly roll pan.

2. Combine the superfine sugar and vanilla seeds in a bowl. In a separate bowl, whisk the egg whites until stiff. Gradually whisk in the vanilla sugar, a spoonful at a time, to form a stiff, glossy meringue mixture.

3. Spread the meringue mixture evenly into the prepared pan. Bake in the oven for 8 minutes. Reduce the oven temperature to 325°F and bake for a further 10 minutes, or until firm to the touch.

4. Turn out onto a sheet of greaseproof paper dusted with sifted powdered sugar. Peel off the lining paper and set aside to cool for 10 minutes.

5. Meanwhile, melt the chocolate in a heat-proof bowl set over a pan of hot water. Remove from the heat and stir in the yogurt, then beat this mixture into the mascarpone cheese in a separate bowl.

6. Spread the chocolate mixture over the meringue and top with the blueberries. Roll up from a long side using the paper underneath to help. Leave wrapped in the paper for at least 1 hour before serving. Remove the paper, dust with sifted powdered sugar, and serve in slices.

RED VELVET Cake

Deep, dark layers of sponge are covered in creamy white frosting to create this truly impressive cake.

MAKES: 10–12 SLICES

6 tablepoons unsalted butter, softened

1½ cups superfine sugar

2 eggs, beaten

1 teaspoon vanilla extract

1½ cups all-purpose flour

3 tablespoons unsweetened cocoa powder

1½ teaspoons baking soda

Pinch of salt

1 tablespoon red food coloring

½ cup buttermilk

1 tablespoon white vinegar

FOR THE FROSTING

6 tablespoons unsalted butter, softened

8 ounces cream cheese

1 pound powdered sugar

1 teaspoon vanilla extract

1 cup pecans, chopped

1. Preheat the oven to 350°F. Grease and flour two 9-inch round cake pans.

2. For the cake, cream the butter and sugar together in a bowl, then beat in the eggs and vanilla extract. Sift the flour, cocoa powder, baking soda, and salt into a separate bowl. Stir the food coloring into the buttermilk.

3. Alternately add the flour and buttermilk mixtures to the creamed mixture. Stir in the vinegar, mixing well. Pour the mixture into the prepared pans, dividing it evenly. Bake in the oven for 30–35 minutes, or until firm to the touch. Cool in the pans for 10 minutes, then turn out onto a wire rack and leave to cool completely.

4. For the frosting, beat the butter and cream cheese together in a bowl. Beat in the powdered sugar and vanilla extract, mixing well, then stir in the pecans. Sandwich the two cakes together with some frosting, then spread the remaining frosting over the top of the cake. Serve in slices.

PRALINE LAYER Cake

Toasted pecan nuts make a truly delicious praline for this tasty layer cake.

MAKES: 8–10 SLICES

4 ounces dark bitter chocolate,
 broken into squares
¼ cup/ ½ stick unsalted butter
2 cups superfine sugar
2 egg yolks
½ cup milk
1⅓ cups self-rising flour
Pinch of salt
½ teaspoon bicarbonate of soda
1 teaspoon vanilla extract
1 cup sugar
¼ cup toasted pecans, chopped
1 cup heavy whipping cream

CAKE TIP
If you don't own a food processor put the praline into a strong plastic bag and crush with a meat mallet or small hammer, or use a pestle and mortar.

1. Preheat the oven to 325°F. Grease and line two 8-inch round cake pans.

2. Melt the chocolate and butter in a large heat-proof bowl set over a pan of gently simmering water, then remove and cool to room temperature. Stir in the caster sugar. Add the egg yolks and half of the milk and mix well.

3. Add the flour, salt, and baking soda and beat for 1 minute, then beat in the remaining milk and the vanilla extract. Pour the mixture into the prepared pans, dividing it evenly.

4. Bake in the oven for 25–30 minutes, or until just firm to the touch. Turn out onto a wire rack and leave to cool.

5. Melt the granulated sugar in a heavy-based saucepan over a low heat. Lightly oil a piece of foil on a baking sheet. When the sugar is golden, stir in the pecans. Pour evenly onto the oiled surface. Leave to cool, then break into small pieces. Process in a blender or food processor to form a fine powder.

6. Whip the cream in a bowl to form soft peaks, then fold in the nut powder. Sandwich the two cakes together with some of the cream icing, then spread the remaining icing over the top of the cake. Cover and refrigerate before serving.

STRAWBERRY Cake with Sliced Almonds

This delightful strawberry cake is a great summertime treat. Substitute best-quality strawberry compote in place of the fresh strawberries, if you prefer.

MAKES: 10–12 SLICES

1¼ cup/2¼ sticks unsalted butter, softened

1¼ cups superfine sugar

2 eggs, beaten

1 teaspoon vanilla extract

Pinch of salt

4 tablespoons sour cream

1 teaspoon baking soda

1½ cups all-purpose flour

1 cup ground almonds

FOR THE FROSTING

1½ cups heavy whipping cream

2 tablespoons powdered sugar

1 teaspoon finely grated lemon zest

4 tablespoons sour cream

4 tablespoons toasted sliced almonds

1 pound strawberries, halved and sliced

1. Preheat the oven to 350°F. Grease and line a deep 9-inch round cake pan.

2. For the cake, cream the butter and sugar together in a bowl until pale and fluffy. Gradually add the eggs, beating well after each addition. Stir in the vanilla extract, salt, and sour cream.

3. Sift the baking soda with the flour, then fold this into the egg mixture together with the ground almonds.

4. Spoon the mixture into the prepared pan and smooth the surface. Bake in the oven for 30–35 minutes, or until golden brown and firm to the touch. Turn out onto a wire rack and leave to cool.

5. For the frosting, whip the cream in a bowl to form soft peaks. Add the powdered sugar, lemon zest, and sour cream, mixing well. Spread the frosting over the top and sides of the cake. Press the sliced almonds around the sides and arrange the strawberry slices on top of the cake. Refrigerate until ready to serve. Serve in slices.

CHOCOLATE & CHESTNUT MACAROON Cake

Drizzle each slice of this tempting cake with melted dark chocolate before serving, if you like.

MAKES: 6–8 SLICES

Scant 2¼ cups powdered sugar
½ teaspoon baking soda
4 large egg whites
Generous 2 cups ground almonds
Scant ½ cup canned sweetened
  chestnut purée
2 tablespoons maple syrup
3 ounces dark bitter chocolate,
  melted
2½ cups mascarpone cheese
Scant ⅔ cups heavy whipping cream
Chocolate curls, to decorate

1. Preheat the oven to 275°F. Line three baking sheets with non-stick baking paper and draw a 7-inch circle on each.

2. Sift the powdered sugar and baking soda into a bowl. In a separate bowl, whisk the egg whites until stiff. Gradually whisk in three-quarters of the powdered sugar until the mixture is stiff and glossy. Mix the remaining powdered sugar into the ground almonds, then fold this into the whisked egg whites. Divide the mixture equally between the three circles on the prepared baking sheets and spread out evenly.

3. Bake in the oven for 10 minutes. Reduce the oven temperature to 225°F and bake for a further 1¼ hours. Transfer to a wire rack to cool, then peel away the paper.

4. Beat the chestnut purée and maple syrup together in a bowl until smooth. Stir in the melted chocolate, then beat in the mascarpone cheese followed by the cream, mixing well.

5. Place a meringue round on a serving plate and spread with half of the chestnut mixture. Place a second meringue round on top and spread that carefully with the remaining chestnut mixture. Top with the remaining meringue round and sprinkle with chocolate curls to decorate.

DARK CHOCOLATE
Cheesecake

A fabulous cheesecake for chocoholics. Use the best-quality chocolate you can find.

MAKES: 10–12 SLICES

7 ounces graham cracker crumbs, crushed

$\frac{1}{4}$ cup/$\frac{1}{2}$ stick unsalted butter, melted

3 x 8-ounce packages cream cheese
Pinch of salt

3 tablespoons cornstarch

1 cup superfine sugar

2 eggs, beaten

2 egg yolks

2 teaspoons vanilla extract

$1\frac{1}{2}$ cups heavy whipping cream

$\frac{1}{2}$ cup sour cream

10 ounces dark bitter chocolate, melted

6 tablespoons unsweetened cocoa powder, sifted, plus extra for dusting

2 tablespoons chocolate shards or curls

1. Preheat the oven to 300°F. Grease a 9-inch springform pan fitted with a flat base.

2. In a small bowl, mix together the graham cracker crumbs and melted butter, then press this mixture evenly into the bottom of the prepared pan. Bake in the oven for 10 minutes, or until lightly browned, then remove from the oven and set aside to cool.

3. Beat the cream cheese in a large bowl until smooth. Add the salt, cornstarch, and sugar and beat together for 1 minute. Gradually add the eggs and egg yolks, beating well to combine. Stir in the vanilla extract. Lightly whip the cream in a separate bowl. Fold the whipped cream and sour cream into the soft cheese mixture.

4. Stir in the melted chocolate and sifted cocoa powder, mixing well. Pour the mixture evenly over the graham cracker crust in the pan. Bake in the oven for 55–60 minutes, or until set at the edges but slightly soft in the center. Turn off the oven, but leave the cheesecake inside for 45 minutes.

5. Remove the cheesecake from the oven and cool to room temperature. Remove from the pan, place on a serving plate, cover with foil, and refrigerate until cold. Decorate the cheesecake with chocolate shards or curls and dust with extra sifted cocoa powder before serving. Serve in slices.

CLASSIC CHEESECAKE
with Blackberry Topping

A delicious fresh blackberry compote tops a classic baked
cheesecake to create this very tempting dessert.

MAKES: **10–12 SLICES**

14 graham crackers, crushed
5 tablespoons unsalted butter,
　melted
3 large eggs, separated
Scant 1 cup superfine sugar
12 ounces cream cheese
Generous ¾ cup sour cream
2 tablespoons cornflour
2 teaspoons vanilla extract
4 teaspoons finely grated lemon zest
FOR THE TOPPING
1 pound fresh blackberries
½ cup superfine sugar
4 teaspoons arrowroot
4 tablespoons blackberry or cherry
　liqueur

1. Preheat the oven to 350°F. Grease and line a 9-inch springform pan
fitted with a flat base. Mix the graham cracker crumbs and melted butter
together and press evenly into the bottom of the prepared pan.

2. Whisk the egg yolks and half of the sugar together in a bowl until
light and fluffy. Gradually add the cream cheese, whisking until smooth.
Add the sour cream, cornstarch, vanilla extract, lemon zest, and the
remaining sugar and mix well.

3. In a separate bowl, whisk the egg whites until stiff, then fold them
into the cheese mixture. Pour the mixture evenly over the graham cracker
crust. Bake in the oven for 1–1¼ hours, or until just set and golden brown
on top. Turn off the oven. Run a knife around the inside edge of the pan,
then leave the cheesecake to cool in the oven with the door ajar.

4. For the topping, put the blackberries in a saucepan with the sugar and
4 tablespoons of water and cook gently for 5 minutes, or until the berries
are soft. Blend the arrowroot with the liqueur and stir into the fruit. Bring
to the boil, then remove from the heat and leave to cool.

5. Remove the cheesecake from the pan and place on a serving plate.
Pour the blackberry mixture evenly over the top. Refrigerate for 4 hours
before serving.

PINEAPPLE UPSIDE-DOWN Cake

CAKE TIP
*Use canned or fresh
apricot, peach,
or pear halves instead
of pineapple rings
if you wish.*

This cake will be much loved for its spectacular appearance when served.

MAKES: 8–10 SLICES

¼ cup/½ stick unsalted butter
Scant ½ cup light brown sugar
15-ounce can pineapple rings in
    natural juice, drained
7 red candied cherries
½ cup toasted sliced almonds
    (optional)
1 cup superfine sugar
3 eggs, separated
5 tablespoons unsweetened
    pineapple juice
½ teaspoon vanilla extract
¼ teaspoon almond extract
1¼ cups self-rising flour, sifted
1 teaspoon baking powder
⅛ teaspoon salt
Evaporated milk or light cream, to
    serve

1. Preheat the oven to 350°F. Grease and line a deep 9-inch round cake pan. Reserve 1 tablespoon of the butter, then melt the rest in a saucepan over a low heat. Pour into the prepared pan and sprinkle the brown sugar evenly over it.

2. Arrange the pineapple rings in the butter-sugar mixture, placing a candied cherry in the center of each ring. Sprinkle the sliced almonds over the top, if using.

3. Cream the reserved butter and the superfine sugar together in a bowl, then gradually beat in the egg yolks. Add the pineapple juice, then the vanilla and almond extracts, mixing well. Sift the flour, baking powder, and salt into the creamed mixture and fold in, mixing well.

4. In a separate bowl, whisk the egg whites until stiff, then fold them into the creamed mixture. Spoon the mixture evenly over the pineapples in the pan.

5. Bake in the oven for 30–35 minutes, or until firm to the touch. Remove the cake from the oven and leave to cool in the pan. Loosen the cake from the pan and invert onto a serving plate so that the pineapple and cherry base is now on top. Serve the cake warm or cold in slices with evaporated milk or light cream.

CHOCOLATE & STRAWBERRY LAYER Cake

A dark chocolate icing complements the sweet fruit filling perfectly in this luxurious chocolate cake. Serve with whipped cream, if you like.

MAKES: 8–10 SLICES

9 ounces dark bitter chocolate, chopped
¾ cup milk
1¼ cup/2 sticks unsalted butter, softened
1 cup dark brown sugar
3 eggs, beaten
1⅓ cup self-rising flour
1 tablespoon baking powder
4 tablespoons unsweetened cocoa powder
4 tablespoons strawberry compote or strawberry jelly
Scant ½ cup powdered sugar

1. Preheat the oven to 325°F. Grease and line two 8-inch round cake pans. Melt 3½ ounces of the chocolate and the milk together in a heat-proof bowl set over a pan of simmering water. Remove from the heat and set aside.

2. Using a hand-held electric mixer, cream a generous ½ cup of the butter and all of the brown sugar together in a bowl until pale and fluffy, then gradually beat in the eggs.

3. Sift the flour, baking powder, and cocoa powder into a separate bowl. Add the flour mixture to the creamed mixture alternately with the chocolate milk. Increase the speed of the mixer for about 30 seconds to mix thoroughly.

4. Divide the mixture evenly between the prepared pans and smooth the surface. Bake in the oven for 25–30 minutes, or until firm to the touch. Turn out onto a wire rack and leave to cool.

5. Melt and cool the remaining chocolate. Sandwich the two cakes together with the strawberry compote or jelly. Cream the remaining butter in a bowl, then beat in the powdered sugar. Pour in the melted, cooled chocolate and mix well. Spread the chocolate icing over the top of the cake. Serve in slices.

DEVIL'S FOOD CAKE with
Choc-Orange Icing

MAKES: 8–10 SLICES

6 ounces dark bitter chocolate,
  broken into squares
$^2/_3$ cup/1$^1/_3$ sticks unsalted butter
$^1/_2$ cup superfine sugar
6 large eggs, separated
$^1/_2$ cup all-purpose flour
$^2/_3$ cup ground almonds

FOR THE FROSTING
Generous $^3/_4$ cup heavy whipping
  cream
7 ounces dark bitter chocolate,
  broken into squares
2 teaspoons finely grated orange zest
Sugar orange slices, to decorate
Sifted powdered sugar, for dusting
  (optional)

1. Preheat the oven to 350°F. Grease and line a deep 8-inch round cake pan.

2. For the cake, melt the chocolate in a heat-proof bowl set over a pan of gently simmering water. Remove and cool slightly. In a separate bowl, beat the butter and half of the sugar together until creamy. Beat in the melted chocolate, then beat in the egg yolks, one at a time.

3. Sift the flour and ground almonds into a separate bowl. In another bowl, whisk the egg whites until stiff, then gradually whisk in the remaining sugar. Stir half of the whisked egg whites into the chocolate mixture to loosen it slightly, then fold in the flour mixture together with the remaining whisked egg whites.

4. Spoon the mixture into the prepared pan and smooth the surface. Bake in the oven for 50–60 minutes, or until a skewer inserted into the center comes out clean. Cool in the pan for 10 minutes, then turn out onto a wire rack and leave to cool completely.

5. To make the frosting, heat the cream in a saucepan until nearly boiling. Remove the pan from the heat, stir in the chocolate until melted, then stir in the orange zest. Keep stirring until thick. Spread the frosting evenly over the top and sides of the cake. Decorate with sugar orange slices, then leave the frosting to set before dusting the cake with sifted powdered sugar, if you like. Serve in slices.

BLUEBERRY CAKE
with Streusel Topping

MAKES: 8–10 SLICES

4 cups all-purpose flour

4 teaspoons baking powder

1 teaspoon salt

6 tablespoons unsalted butter, softened

1¼ cups superfine sugar

2 eggs, lightly beaten

1½ teaspoons vanilla extract

1¼ cups milk

3 cups fresh blueberries

FOR THE TOPPING

⅔ cup superfine sugar

⅓ cup light brown sugar

6 tablespoons unsalted butter, softened

⅔ cup all-purpose flour

½ cup toasted walnuts or pecans, chopped

1½ teaspoons ground cinnamon

½ teaspoon freshly grated nutmeg

½ teaspoon salt

FOR THE FILLING

12 ounces cream cheese, softened

⅓ cup superfine sugar

1 egg

Finely grated zest of 1 lemon

1–2 tablespoons fresh lemon juice

1 teaspoon vanilla extract

1. Preheat the oven to 375°F. Generously grease a 11 x 13-inch ovenproof glass baking dish.

2. To make the topping, rub the sugars, butter, and flour together in a bowl until the mixture forms coarse crumbs. Stir in the nuts, cinnamon, nutmeg, and salt. Refrigerate until ready to use.

3. To make the filling, using a hand-held electric mixer, beat the cream cheese in a bowl until creamy. Gradually beat in the sugar. Beat in the egg, lemon zest and juice, and vanilla extract. Set aside.

4. For the cake, sift the flour, baking powder, and salt into a bowl. Set aside. In a separate bowl, beat the butter until creamy. Gradually beat in the sugar, then beat in the eggs and vanilla extract. Fold in the flour mixture alternately with the milk, mixing well. Fold in the blueberries.

5. Spread a little less than half of the cake mixture over the base of the prepared dish. Gently spread the filling evenly over the cake mixture, then sprinkle a quarter of the topping over the filling. Drop spoonfuls of the remaining cake mixture over the top and spread evenly. Sprinkle the remaining topping over the surface.

6. Bake in the oven for about 1 hour, or until crunchy and golden on top. Transfer to a wire rack and leave to cool. Cut into squares and serve warm or at room temperature.

BLACK CHERRY & CHOCOLATE Cake

CAKE TIP
Use fresh cherries when they are in season instead of candied cherries for a stylish decoration.

This classic Black Forest gâteau is sure to be a family favorite.

MAKES: 10–12 SLICES

2 x 15-ounce cans pitted black cherries, drained
1 cup rum
6 eggs
1 cup superfine sugar
1 cup self-rising flour
5 tablespoons unsweetened cocoa powder
2 cups heavy whipping cream
3 tablespoons black cherry jelly
4 ounces dark bitter chocolate, grated
12 dark red candied cherries, to decorate

1. Preheat the oven to 400°F. Grease and line two 9-inch round cake pans. Put the cherries in a bowl and pour over half of the rum. Set aside.

2. Put the eggs and sugar, less 3 tablespoons, in a large heat-proof bowl set over a pan of simmering water. Using a hand-held electric mixer, whisk for 15–20 minutes, or until the mixture is pale, creamy, and thick enough to leave a trail Remove from the heat. Sift the flour and cocoa powder over the whisked egg mixture and fold in gently but thoroughly.

3. Pour the mixture into the prepared pans, dividing it evenly. Bake in the oven for 12–15 minutes, or until just firm to the touch. Turn out onto a wire rack and leave to cool.

4. Whip the cream in a bowl to form soft peaks. Whisk in the remaining rum and the 3 tablespoons of sugar. Brush each of the sponge cakes with the rum that the cherries have been soaking in, then spread the jelly evenly over one of the sponge cakes. Top this sponge cake with one third of the cream and the cherries. Place the other sponge cake on top, then cover the top of the cake with cream, reserving some for decoration.

5. Sprinkle the top of the cake with the grated chocolate, then pipe 12 rosettes of cream around the top edge of the cake. Top with the candied cherries. Refrigerate for 45 minutes before serving.

CAPPUCCINO TRUFFLE Cake

This delicious coffee and chocolate combination is more like a cold soufflé than a cake. Serve with whipped cream, if you like.

MAKES: 6–8 SLICES

1 tablespoon instant coffee powder
Scant ²/₃ cup boiling water
¹/₂ cup stoned dried prunes, chopped
4 tablespoons Tia Maria, or other coffee liqueur
6 ounces dark bitter chocolate, broken into squares
¹/₂ cup/1 stick unsalted butter
5 eggs, separated
¹/₂ cup superfine sugar
1 teaspoon vanilla extract
1 tablespoon cornstarch
Unsweetened cocoa powder, for dusting

1. Dissolve the coffee powder in the boiling water in a small bowl, then pour over the prunes in a bowl. Stir in the Tia Maria. Leave to soak overnight.

2. Preheat the oven to 325°F. Grease and line an 8-inch springform pan fitted with a flat base.

3. Melt the chocolate and butter in a heat-proof bowl set over a pan of hot water. Remove from the heat.

4. Using a hand-held electric mixer, whisk the egg yolks and sugar together in a separate heat-proof bowl set over a pan of simmering water, until the mixture is very thick and creamy. Remove from the heat.

5. Drain any excess liquid from the prunes. Stir the vanilla extract, drained prunes, and melted chocolate into the creamy mixture and set aside.

6. With clean beaters, whisk the egg whites in a clean bowl until stiff. Whisk in the cornstarch, then fold this into the chocolate mixture. Pour the mixture evenly into the prepared pan. Bake in the oven for 50 minutes, or until springy to the touch.

7. Remove the cake from the oven and leave it to cool completely in the pan. Turn the cake out onto a serving plate and dust with sifted cocoa powder. Serve in slices.

ICE CREAM Cake

MAKES: 10–12 SLICES

1½ cups superfine sugar

1 cup self-rising flour

8 egg whites

1¼ teaspoons cream of tartar

Pinch of salt

1 teaspoon almond extract

½ teaspoon vanilla extract

6–8 maraschino cherries (optional)

Sifted powdered sugar, for dusting

FOR THE MELBA SAUCE & FILLING

¾ cup superfine sugar

2 cups fresh raspberries, puréed and chilled

Scoops of ice cream, preferably vanilla—to fill the center

1 x 15-ounce can peach slices in fruit juice, drained

CAKE TIP

As an alternative, use mint chocolate chip ice cream and dust the top of the cake with a combination of sifted powdered sugar and unsweetened cocoa powder. Serve with fresh strawberries and a hot chocolate sauce.

1. Preheat the oven to 350°F. For the cake, sift the superfine sugar twice into a bowl. In a separate bowl, sift the flour four times. Set both aside.

2. Whisk the egg whites in another bowl until frothy. Add the cream of tartar and salt, and continue to whisk until the mixture forms soft peaks. Sprinkle 2 tablespoons of the superfine sugar over the egg white peaks and whisk until blended. Repeat the process until the superfine sugar is all used up.

3. Whisk in the almond and vanilla extracts. Using a rubber spatula, fold in the flour, ⅓ cup at a time. Cut the maraschino cherries into quarters, if using, and fold them into the cake mixture. Spoon the mixture into an ungreased 9-inch fluted ring pan. Cut through the mixture with a knife to get rid of any air bubbles, then level the surface. Bake in the oven for 40–60 minutes, or until the top turns light brown.

4. Invert the cake onto a wire rack and leave to cool in the pan for 1 hour. Run a sharp knife around the edges of the pan to loosen the cake before transferring it to a serving plate.

5. Meanwhile, to make the melba sauce, combine the sugar and ½ cup boiling water in a saucepan and boil for 10 minutes. Remove the pan from the heat and set aside to cool, then add the raspberry purée. Press the mixture through a fine mesh strainer and refrigerate.

6. To serve, fill the center recess of the cake with the ice cream and peaches. Pour some of the melba sauce over the ice cream, taking care to avoid soaking the cake, then serve the rest separately. Dust the cake with sifted powdered sugar and serve immediately in slices.

MIDDLE EASTERN ORANGE Cake

To flavor this moist and delicious cake, 2 whole oranges, including the pith and peel, are used. This gives it a really intense citrus taste and makes it perfect to serve as a dessert with crème fraîche or whipped cream.

MAKES: 10–12 SLICES

2 small oranges
5 eggs
³/₄ cup light brown sugar
2¹/₃ cups ground almonds
¹/₂ cup all-purpose flour
1 teaspoon baking powder
2 tablespoons sliced almonds
Sifted powdered sugar, for dusting

1. Put the whole oranges in a saucepan and cover with water. Bring to the boil, then cover and simmer for about 1¹/₂ hours, or until the oranges are really soft. Remove the pan from the heat, drain, and set aside to cool. Halve the oranges and remove the seeds, then purée the oranges in a blender or food processor. Measure 1¹/₄ cups of the pulp and discard the rest.

2. Preheat the oven to 350°F. Grease and line a deep 9-inch round cake pan. Using a hand-held electric mixer, whisk the eggs and sugar together in a large heat-proof bowl set over a pan of simmering water until the mixture is pale, creamy, and thick enough to leave a trail on the surface when the whisk is lifted. Remove from the heat.

3. Fold the measured orange pulp into the whisked egg mixture, together with the ground almonds, flour, and baking powder, mixing well. Pour the mixture evenly into the prepared pan, then scatter the sliced almonds over the top.

4. Bake in the oven for 1 hour, or until a skewer inserted into the center comes out clean. Cool in the pan for 10 minutes, then turn out onto a wire rack. Dust with sifted powdered sugar. Serve warm or cold in slices.

PLUM & AMARETTI
Sponge Cake

Crushed amaretti add an interesting crunch to this sheetcake and the almond flavor works incredibly well with the plums. Serve with crème fraîche or vanilla ice cream for dessert.

MAKES: 24 SQUARES

¾ cup/1½ sticks unsalted butter, softened

Scant 1 cup superfine sugar

3 large eggs

1½ cups self-rising flour, sifted

2 teaspoons finely grated lemon zest

1 tablespoon fresh lemon juice

6 plums, halved and stoned

1 ounce amaretti cookies, coarsely crushed

1 tablespoon demerara sugar, for sprinkling

1. Preheat the oven to 350°F. Grease and line an 11 x 7-inch cake pan.

2. Cream the butter and superfine sugar together in a bowl until pale and fluffy. Gradually add the eggs, beating well after each addition. Sift the flour over the creamed mixture and fold in together with the lemon zest and juice, mixing well.

3. Spoon the mixture into the prepared pan and smooth the surface. Arrange the plum halves, cut-side down, over the top, then sprinkle with the crushed amaretti and demerara sugar.

4. Bake in the oven for 45–50 minutes, or until risen and golden brown. Cool slightly in the pan, then turn out onto a wire rack, invert the cake so that the plums are on top and leave to cool. Serve warm or cold cut into squares or slices.

CAKE TIP

When in season, use greengages instead of plums, or try blackberry and apple to ring the changes.

WHIPPED CREAM
Cheesecake

An exceptionally light and creamy cheesecake that makes a flamboyant centerpiece.

MAKES: 12–14 SLICES

7 ounces graham crackers, crushed
¼ cup/½ stick unsalted butter, melted
3 x 8-ounce packages cream cheese
Pinch of salt
3 tablespoons cornstarch
1 cup superfine sugar
2 eggs, beaten
2 egg yolks
2 teaspoons vanilla extract
1 teaspoon seeds from a vanilla bean (optional)
2½ cups heavy whipping cream
Fruit, to decorate

1. Preheat the oven to 300°F. Grease a 9-inch springform pan fitted with a flat base. Mix together the cracker crumbs and melted butter, and press evenly into the bottom of the prepared pan. Bake in the oven for 10 minutes, or until lightly browned. Remove from the oven and set aside to cool.

2. Beat the cream cheese in a large bowl until soft and smooth. Add the salt, cornstarch, and sugar and beat for 1 minute. Gradually add the eggs and egg yolks, beating well to combine. Stir in the vanilla extract and vanilla seeds, if using.

3. In a separate bowl, whip the cream to form soft peaks, then fold half of the whipped cream into the cheese mixture. Refrigerate the remaining cream. Pour the cheese mixture evenly over the graham cracker crust. Bake in the oven for 50–60 minutes, or until set at the edges but slightly soft in the center.

4. Turn off the oven, leave the cheesecake inside, and leave the door ajar. Cool in the oven for 30 minutes. Remove the cheesecake and cool to room temperature, then remove it from the pan, place on a serving plate, cover with foil, and refrigerate until cold.

5. Spread the remaining whipped cream evenly over the top of the cheesecake and decorate with your favorite fruit. Serve in slices.

PEACH Cake

The peach halves in this recipe keep the cake moist and fruity—
ideal for a family dessert, served with cream or ice cream.

MAKES: 10–12 SLICES

¾ cup/1½ sticks unsalted butter,
   softened
Scant 1 cup superfine sugar
3 eggs, beaten
2 cups ground almonds
⅔ cup self-rising flour
2 teaspoons vanilla extract
1 x 15-ounce can peach halves in
   fruit juice, drained
Sifted powdered sugar, to dust

1. Preheat the oven to 350°F. Grease and line a deep 9-inch round cake pan.

2. Cream the butter and powdered sugar together in a bowl until pale
and fluffy, then gradually add the eggs, beating well after each addition.
Stir in the ground almonds, flour, and vanilla extract.

3. Spoon the mixture into the prepared pan and smooth the surface.
Arrange the peach halves, cut-side down, over the top.

4. Bake in the oven for 35–40 minutes, or until risen and golden brown.
Cool in the pan for 10 minutes, then turn out
onto a wire rack, invert the cake
so that the peaches are on
top and leave to cool
completely. Dust with
the sifted powdered sugar.
Serve in slices.

SUGAR & SPICE Cake

Warming spices richly flavor this easy-to-prepare cake, which tastes great as a light dessert served with coffee.

MAKES: 12–14 SLICES

3/4 cup/1 1/2 sticks unsalted butter, softened
1 1/4 cups light brown sugar
2 eggs, beaten
1 2/3 cups all-purpose flour
1/2 teaspoon baking powder
1 teaspoon ground cinnamon
1/2 teaspoon freshly grated nutmeg
1/2 teaspoon ground ginger
Pinch of salt
1–2 tablespoons milk
1 tablespoon demerara sugar

1. Preheat the oven to 350°F. Grease and line a 10-inch loaf pan.

2. Beat the butter in a bowl until pale and creamy, then add the soft brown sugar and beat for a further 3–4 minutes. Gradually add the eggs, beating well to mix. Sift the flour, baking powder, cinnamon, nutmeg, ginger, and salt over the creamed mixture and fold in, gradually adding the milk at the same time.

3. Pour the mixture evenly into the prepared pan, then sprinkle the demerara sugar over the top. Bake in the oven for 50–55 minutes, or until firm to the touch and a skewer inserted into the center comes out clean. Cool in the pan for 5 minutes, then turn out onto a wire rack and leave to cool completely. Serve in slices.

CAKE TIP
This cake can be cut into slices and frozen so a few slices can be defrosted and used as a quick dessert with fresh fruit and ice cream.

YEASTED SOUR CREAM Cake

This tasty loaf cake creates an ideal sweet treat to enjoy after a main course or supper.

MAKES: 12–14 SLICES

1 teaspoon dried active yeast
$\frac{1}{2}$ cup warmed water
2 cups all-purpose flour
5 tablespoons sour cream
$\frac{1}{3}$ cup cream cheese
$\frac{2}{3}$ cup/$1\frac{1}{3}$ sticks unsalted butter, melted
$\frac{1}{2}$ cup superfine sugar
2 eggs, beaten
2 egg yolks
1 teaspoon ground cinnamon
4 tablespoons sliced almonds
3 tablespoons apricot jelly
3 tablespoons powdered sugar
1 tablespoon lemon juice

1. Grease a 10-inch loaf pan. Dissolve the yeast in the warmed water in a large bowl, then stir in 2 tablespoons of the flour. Stand in a warm place for about 10 minutes, or until the yeast starts to froth.

2. Mix the sour cream, cream cheese and melted butter together in a separate bowl, then stir in the superfine sugar, eggs, and egg yolks. Set aside.

3. When the yeast has started to work, add the remaining flour and the cinnamon to the yeast mixture and stir in. Add the sour cream mixture and mix to form a soft dough. Shape the dough into a ball and place it in an oiled bowl. Cover with a clean damp dish towel and leave to rise in a warm place for about 1 hour, or until doubled in size.

4. Knead the sliced almonds into the dough, then shape the dough into an oblong and place it in the prepared pan. Leave to rise again for 20–30 minutes. Meanwhile, preheat the oven to 375°F.

5. Bake the loaf in the oven for 25–30 minutes, or until golden. Turn out onto a wire rack and leave to cool.

6. Gently heat the apricot jam with 3 tablespoons of water in a small saucepan. Brush the apricot glaze evenly over the top of the loaf cake. In a small bowl, combine the powdered sugar and lemon juice, then drizzle the lemon icing evenly over the loaf cake. Serve in slices.

RASPBERRY SOUFFLÉ Gateau

MAKES: 10–12 SLICES

6 tablespoons unsalted butter, melted

2 cups graham crackers, crushed

¾ cup superfine sugar

4 cups frozen raspberries

1 tablespoon powdered gelatine

1¼ cups heavy whipping cream

3 egg whites

Pinch of cream of tartar

1¼ cups heavy cream, whipped to form soft peaks

2 cups fresh raspberries

3–4 tablespoons seedless raspberry jam, warmed

1. Preheat the oven to 350°F. Grease a 9-inch springform pan fitted with a flat base. Combine the melted butter, graham cracker crumbs, and ¼ cup of the sugar in a bowl. Press the crumb mixture evenly into the base of the prepared pan. Bake in the oven for 10 minutes, then remove from the oven and set aside to cool.

2. Combine the frozen raspberries with 3 tablespoons of water in a pan and simmer gently until the raspberries are soft. Process the mixture in a blender or food processor for 30 seconds, then strain to remove the seeds.

3. Sprinkle the gelatine over 3 tablespoons of hot water. Dissolve in a heat-proof bowl set over a pan of simmering water. Stir the dissolved gelatine into the raspberry pulp. Set aside.

4. In a separate bowl, whip the heavy whipping cream to form soft peaks, then fold this through the raspberry pulp. In another bowl, whisk the egg whites until soft peaks form. Whisk in the cream of tartar and half of the remaining sugar, then whisk in the remaining sugar until the mixture is thick and glossy.

5. Fold the whisked egg white mixture through the raspberry and cream mixture, then spoon the mixture evenly over the graham cracker crust. Chill in the refrigerator for 2–3 hours, or until set, then remove the gateau from the pan and place it on a serving plate.

6. Pipe the whipped heavy cream decoratively around the top edge of the gateau. Arrange the fresh raspberries in the center on top and spoon the warmed jelly evenly over the raspberries. Serve in slices.

APRICOT FRANGIPANE Cake

This dessert cake has a wonderful consistency and flavor. Combining apricots and almonds is nothing new, but the partnership works so well that it is always worth repeating.

MAKES: 8–10 SLICES

½ cup/1 stick unsalted butter or margarine, softened

½ cup superfine sugar

½ teaspoon almond extract

¾ cup all-purpose flour

1 teaspoon baking powder

½ cup ground almonds

2 eggs

8 fresh ripe apricots, halved and stoned

2 tablespoons apricot jelly

¼ cup sliced almonds, to decorate

1. Preheat the oven to 350°F. Grease and line a 9-inch springform pan fitted with a flat base.

2. Cream the butter or margarine and sugar together in a bowl until pale and fluffy. Beat in the almond extract. Set aside. Combine the flour, baking powder, and ground almonds in a separate bowl. In another bowl, whisk the eggs until they are pale, creamy, and thick.

3. Fold the dry ingredients into the creamed mixture alternately with the whisked eggs. Spoon the mixture into the prepared pan and smooth the surface, then arrange the apricot halves, cut-side down, over the top.

4. Bake in the oven for 35 minutes, or until risen and golden. Cool in the pan for 10 minutes, then carefully remove the cake from the pan and place it on a wire rack, apricot side up. Cool for a further 10 minutes.

5. Melt the apricot jelly with 2 teaspoons of water in a small saucepan over a low heat. Press the mixture through a strainer into a bowl. Brush the top of the warm cake with the apricot glaze, then scatter the sliced almonds on top. Serve warm or cold in slices.

CANDIED FRUIT Cassata

MAKES: 8–10 SLICES

FOR THE SPONGE FINGERS
¾ cup all-purpose flour
4 large eggs, separated
½ cup superfine sugar
1 teaspoon vanilla extract
Sifted powdered sugar, for dusting

FOR THE CASSATA
6 tablespoons sweet Marsala
2 cups ricotta cheese
1 cup powdered sugar, sifted
2½ ounces semi-sweet chocolate,
　finely chopped
⅔ cup mixed candied fruits, chopped
¾ cup toasted sliced almonds,
　chopped

1. Preheat the oven to 350°F. Grease and flour two baking sheets. Sift the flour into a bowl and set aside.

2. Using a hand-held electric mixer, whisk the egg yolks and half of the superfine sugar together in a large heat-proof bowl set over a pan of simmering water, until the mixture is creamy and very thick. Whisk in the vanilla extract. In a separate bowl, whisk the egg whites until stiff. Whisk in the remaining superfine sugar until the meringue mixture is thick and glossy.

3. Use a large metal spoon to gently fold the meringue mixture and then the sifted flour into the whisked egg yolks. Spoon the mixture into a piping bag fitted with a plain ¾-inch tip and quickly pipe 4 inch lengths of the mixture in lines on the prepared baking sheets. Dust the tops with sifted powdered sugar and bake in the oven for 15–18 minutes, or until pale golden and just firm to the touch. Transfer to a wire rack and leave to cool.

4. To assemble the cassata, line a 1½-quart soufflé dish with plastic wrap. Use half of the sponge fingers to line the bottom of the prepared dish, cutting them to fit where necessary. Dip these sponge fingers into the Marsala and arrange in the bottom of the dish. Cut the remaining sponge fingers to fit around the sides, then dip each of these in the Marsala and arrange them around the sides of the dish.

5. Mix together the remaining cassata ingredients and spoon evenly into the dish. Top with any leftover pieces of sponge fingers and drizzle over any remaining Marsala. Cover and refrigerate overnight. Invert the dessert onto a serving plate, dust with sifted powdered sugar and serve in slices.

HEALTHY &
SPECIAL DIET
CAKES

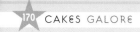

PEAR & RASPBERRY Cake

A full and fruity cake, which is best kept in a cool place after
baking. The mixture fills the pan before baking but don't worry
as it does not rise too much.

MAKES: **12–14 SLICES**

2 cups firm pears (2 medium), peeled,
   cored, and chopped
1 cup dried sweetened cranberries
1 cup raspberry juice or mixed berry
   juice
2 cups mixed fresh raspberries and
   blueberries
1 cup gluten-free flour
1 cup corn flour or fine cornmeal
2 teaspoons gluten-free baking
   powder
2 large egg whites
1 cup unrefined superfine sugar
Sifted unrefined powdered sugar, to
   decorate (optional)

NUTRITIONAL NOTE
This cake is suitable for low fat,
gluten-free, wheat-free, dairy-
free, and nut-free diets.

1. Preheat the oven to 350°F. Grease and line a 10-inch loaf pan. Put the
pears, cranberries, and fruit juice into a saucepan and bring the mixture to
a boil over a medium heat. Remove the pan from the heat and set aside
to cool.

2. Put the cooled fruit and juice into a large bowl and add the raspberries
and blueberries. Sift the gluten-free flour, corn flour or cornmeal, and
baking powder together and stir into the fruit mixture.

3. In a separate bowl, whisk the egg whites until stiff, then gradually whisk
in the superfine sugar to make a thick, glossy meringue mixture. Fold a little
of the meringue into the fruit mixture to loosen it, then fold in the
remainder. Spoon the mixture into the prepared pan and smooth the surface.

4. Bake in the oven for about $1\frac{1}{4}$ hours, or until slightly risen, golden
brown, and firm to the touch. Cool in the pan for about 20 minutes, then
turn out onto a wire rack and leave to cool completely. Dust with a little
sifted powdered sugar, if you like, and serve in slices.

STICKY
Gingerbread

To make this cake even more special, you can make a quick glaze with 1¼ cup unrefined powdered sugar and a little warm water and trickle it over the cake when cold.

MAKES: 16 SQUARES

½ cup dairy-free margarine
¾ cup dark sugar
2 large eggs, beaten
¾ cup rice flour
¾ cup potato flour
1 teaspoon baking soda
⅓ cup molasses, warmed
⅓ cup light corn syrup, warmed
1 tablespoon ground ginger
⅔ cup raisins
½ cup candied ginger, chopped

1. Preheat the oven to 325°F. Grease and line a deep 8-inch square cake pan.

2. Beat the margarine and sugar together in a bowl until creamy. Gradually add the eggs, beating well after each addition. Add all the remaining ingredients and beat together until well mixed. Pour the mixture evenly into the prepared pan.

3. Bake in the oven for 1 hour, then test by inserting a skewer into the center—it should come out clean. If the cake needs further baking, reduce the oven temperature to 300°F, and bake until firm. Cool in the pan for about 20 minutes, then turn out onto a wire rack and leave to cool completely. Cut into slices or squares to serve.

NUTRITIONAL NOTE
This cake is suitable for gluten-free, wheat-free, dairy-free, and nut-free diets.

SCENTED TEA Loaf

Lady Grey Tea has a lovely scent of orange and lemon peel, but if you can't find it you can substitute Earl Grey Tea. This cake improves after a few days.

MAKES: 12–14 SLICES

½ cup dairy-free margarine

1 cup unrefined superfine sugar

1 cup strong brewed Lady Grey Tea

1½ cups luxury mixed dried fruit

⅔ cup rice flour

⅔ cup potato flour

2 teaspoons gluten-free baking powder

Finely grated zest and juice of 1 orange

Finely grated zest of I lemon

1 egg, beaten

2 tablespoons sieved apricot jelly, warmed

1. Preheat the oven to 350°F. Grease and line a 10-inch loaf pan.

2. Put the margarine, sugar, tea, and dried fruit into a saucepan and bring to a boil. Simmer gently for 5 minutes, stirring occasionally. Remove the pan from the heat and set aside to cool for 15 minutes.

3. Sift the flours and baking powder into a bowl. Add the flour mixture, orange zest and juice, lemon zest, and egg to the fruit mixture and stir to mix well. Pour the mixture evenly into the prepared pan.

4. Bake in the oven for 1–1½ hours, or until well risen and firm to the touch. Remove the cake from the oven and brush the top of the hot cake with the apricot jelly.

5. Cool in the pan for about 20 minutes, then turn out onto a wire rack and leave to cool completely. Serve in slices.

NUTRITIONAL NOTE
This cake is suitable for gluten-free, wheat-free, nut-free, and dairy-free diets.

CAKE TIP
All gluten-free cakes can be improved by adding ¼ teaspoon Xanthum gum to every ⅔ cup flour. Readily available from health food stores, it helps increase volume and storage time.

OLIVE OIL Cake

Use an extra-virgin olive oil for this cake but make sure it is a mild one. This delicious cake is also good served with fresh fruit.

MAKES: 10–12 SLICES

1¼ cups unrefined superfine sugar
Finely grated zest of 2 lemons
4 eggs, beaten
Generous 1 cup gluten-free flour
2 teaspoons gluten-free baking powder
Generous ½ cup ground almonds
5 tablespoons rice milk
⅔ cup mild extra-virgin olive oil
6 tablespoons dairy-free margarine, melted
Juice of 1 lemon
¼ cup pine nuts, lightly toasted

1. Preheat the oven to 350°F. Grease and line a 9-inch springform pan fitted with a flat base.

2. Put the sugar, lemon zest, and eggs into a large bowl and whisk together until the mixture is pale, creamy, and thick enough to leave a trail on the surface when the whisk is lifted. Sift the flour and baking powder into a separate bowl, then stir in the ground almonds.

3. Whisk the rice milk, olive oil, melted margarine, and lemon juice into the egg mixture, then fold in the flour mixture until just combined. Pour the mixture evenly into the prepared pan and sprinkle with the pine nuts.

4. Bake in the oven for 30–40 minutes, or until golden brown and firm to the touch. Remove the cake from the oven and leave to cool completely in the pan, then turn out and serve in slices.

NUTRITIONAL NOTE
This cake is suitable for gluten-free, wheat-free, and dairy-free diets.

MOIST CHOCOLATE Cake

This tasty cake is very much like a chocolate brownie. You can use pecans or macadamia nuts instead of walnuts or leave them out altogether if you are allergic to nuts.

MAKES: 12–14 SLICES

²/₃ cup gluten-free flour

2 tablespoons rice flour

4 tablespoons unsweetened cocoa powder

¹/₄ teaspoon baking soda

¹/₂ teaspoon gluten-free baking powder

1 cup walnuts, chopped

6 ounces dark bitter or semi-sweet chocolate, broken into squares

Scant ¹/₂ cup dairy-free margarine

4 eggs

1¹/₂ cups unrefined superfine sugar

2 teaspoons vanilla extract

FOR THE FROSTING

¹/₂ cup coconut milk

4 ounces dark bitter or semi-sweet chocolate, chopped

3 tablespoons dairy-free margarine

¹/₄ cup walnuts, chopped (optional)

NUTRITIONAL NOTE
This cake is suitable for gluten-free and dairy-free diets.

1. Preheat the oven to 350°F. Grease and line a 9-inch round loose-bottomed cake pan.

2. For the cake, sift the flour, rice flour, cocoa powder, baking soda, and baking powder into a bowl. Stir in the walnuts. Set aside.

3. Melt the chocolate and margarine together in a heat-proof bowl set over a pan of hot water. Remove from the heat and set aside to cool slightly. In a separate bowl, beat the eggs, sugar, and vanilla extract together. Stir in the melted chocolate mixture, then add this to the flour mixture and stir together until just combined.

4. Spoon the mixture into the prepared pan and smooth the surface. Bake in the oven for about 30 minutes, or until firm to the touch. Remove the cake from the oven and cool in the pan for about 20 minutes, then turn out carefully and place on a serving plate. Set aside to cool completely.

5. To make the frosting, put the coconut milk in a small saucepan and bring to a boil. Remove the pan from the heat and immediately add the chocolate and margarine to the hot milk. Stir well until smooth, then leave to cool until the mixture is of a thick spreading consistency. Spread the frosting evenly over the top of the cake. Sprinkle with chopped walnuts, if you like, then leave until set. Serve in slices.

ORANGE CAKE
with Rosemary Glaze

This is a tasty cut-and-come-again cake that is good served with tea or coffee.

MAKES: 8–10 SLICES

Generous 1 cup gluten-free flour

2 tablespoons rice flour

¼ teaspoon baking soda

¼ teaspoon gluten-free baking powder

Scant ½ cup dairy-free margarine

1 cup unrefined sugar

Finely grated zest of 1 orange

2 eggs, beaten

½ teaspoon vanilla extract

3 tablespoons unsweetened orange juice

3 tablespoons rice milk

5 tablespoons coconut milk

FOR THE SYRUP

5 tablespoons unsweetened orange juice

2 tablespoons unrefined superfine sugar

Sprig of fresh rosemary, washed and patted dry

> **NUTRITIONAL NOTE**
> This cake is suitable for gluten-free and dairy-free diets.

1. Preheat the oven to 350°F. Grease and line a 5-inch loaf pan. For the cake, sift the flours, baking soda, and baking powder into a bowl and set aside. In a separate bowl, beat together the margarine, sugar, and orange zest. Gradually add the eggs, beating well after each addition.

2. In another bowl, mix together the vanilla extract, orange juice, rice milk, and coconut milk. Stir this thoroughly into the egg mixture alternately with the flour mixture. Do not over-mix.

3. Spoon the mixture into the prepared pan and smooth the surface. Bake in the oven for about 1 hour, or until a skewer inserted into the center comes out clean.

4. Meanwhile, make the syrup. Put the orange juice and sugar into a small saucepan. Strip the leaves from the sprig of rosemary and add them to the pan. Bring to the boil, stirring, then boil for about 2 minutes, or until syrupy.

5. Remove the cake from the oven. Prick the top of the hot cake all over with a skewer or fork and slowly pour over the syrup. Leave the cake in the pan until completely cold, then turn out and serve in slices.

MANGO & PASSION FRUIT Roll

MAKES: 8–10 SLICES

4 eggs, separated

1 cup powdered sugar, plus extra for dusting

1 tablespoon orange flower water

4 tablespoons rice flour

4 tablespoons potato flour

1 teaspoon gluten-free baking powder

FOR THE FILLING

1¼ cups sheep's or goat's natural yogurt or whipped soy cream

½ large mango, peeled, pitted, and chopped

¼ small papaya, peeled, seeded, and chopped

1 passion fruit

FOR THE DECORATION

½ large mango, peeled, pitted, and thinly sliced

1 passion fruit, cut in half

NUTRITIONAL NOTE
This cake is suitable for low fat, wheat-free, gluten-free, nut-free, and dairy-free diets.

1. Preheat the oven to 375°F. Grease and line a 12½ x 9-inch jelly roll pan, then grease the lining paper.

2. For the cake, put the egg whites in a bowl and whisk until the mixture forms soft peaks. Sift half of the powdered sugar over the top and whisk in.

3. In a separate bowl, whisk the egg yolks with the remaining powdered sugar until the mixture is pale and very thick. Stir in the orange flower water. Sift the flours and baking powder over the top and fold in. Using a metal spoon, fold in the whisked egg whites mixture, one third at a time.

4. Spoon the mixture into the pan, spreading it evenly. Bake in the oven for about 12–15 minutes, or until springy to the touch. Sprinkle a little extra sifted powdered sugar over a large sheet of non-stick baking paper and turn out the sponge cake onto the paper. Remove the lining paper, trim off any firm edges, then loosely roll up the cake with the paper inside and leave to cool on a wire rack.

5. For the filling, carefully unroll the cake and spread the yogurt or soy cream evenly over the cake. Sprinkle with the chopped mango and papaya. Halve the passion fruit and spoon the juice and seeds over the fruit.

6. Carefully roll up the cake, place it on a serving plate and dust with extra sifted powdered sugar. Decorate with slices of mango and the juice and seeds of the passion fruit. Serve in slices.

FEEL GOOD Cake

This cake is reportedly good for combating menopausal symptoms.
It will keep well for up to 1 week in the refrigerator.

MAKES: 8–10 SLICES

²/₃ cup soy flour

²/₃ cup whole-wheat flour

1 cup rolled oats

³/₄ cup flax seeds

¹/₂ cup sesame seeds

¹/₂ cup sliced almonds

3 tablespoons sunflower oil

1¹/₄ cups dried fruit such as raisins
or chopped dried apricots or
a mixture

1 teaspoon ground cinnamon

¹/₂ teaspoon ground ginger

Pinch of freshly grated nutmeg

³/₄ cup soy milk

1 tablespoon malt extract

2 tablespoons clear honey

1. Preheat the oven to 350°F. Grease and line a 5-inch loaf pan.

2. Put all of the ingredients into a large bowl and mix together thoroughly. Set aside to soak for 30 minutes. If the mixture is then too stiff, stir in a little more soy milk.

3. Spoon the mixture into the prepared pan and smooth the surface. Bake in the oven for about 1¹/₄ hours, or until a skewer inserted into the center comes out clean.

4. Cool in the pan for 5–10 minutes, then turn out onto a wire rack and leave to cool completely. This cake is best stored in the refrigerator.

CAKE TIP
Any dried fruit can be used in this cake, try prunes, figs, sweetened dried blueberries or cranberries, dates, apples, and even exotic fruits such as mango or papaya.

ROSEWATER MERINGUE Cake

This meringue is beautifully scented with rosewater and makes a great dessert or afternoon treat. The meringue can be made in advance but assemble the cake just before serving.

MAKES: 6–8 SLICES

4 large egg whites
1¼ cups superfine sugar
2 teaspoons cornstarch
1 teaspoon white wine vinegar
A few drops of rosewater essence

FOR THE FILLING & TOPPING
1¼ cups low-fat raspberry or strawberry fromage frais
⅔ cup fresh strawberries or raspberries
Crystallized rose petals, to decorate

NUTRITIONAL NOTE
This cake is very low in fat and suitable for wheat-free and nut-free diets.

1. Preheat the oven to 300°F. Grease two 8-inch round cake pans and line the bottoms with non-stick baking paper or oiled foil.

2. Whisk the egg whites in a large bowl until the mixture forms soft peaks. Gradually whisk in the sugar a little at a time. Whisk in the cornstarch and vinegar and add a few drops of rosewater essence to taste.

3. Spoon the mixture into the prepared pans, dividing it evenly, then smooth the surface. Bake in the oven for 1½ hours, then turn the oven off and leave the meringues inside until cold.

4. Just before serving, remove the meringues from the pans and peel off the lining paper. Place one meringue round on a serving plate. Spread the fromage frais evenly over the meringue and arrange the strawberries or raspberries on top. Place the second meringue round on top and sprinkle with crystallized rose petals to decorate. Serve immediately, cut into slices.

BERRY LEMON POLENTA Cake

This cake can also be made in an 8-inch pie dish and served as a dessert with some yogurt or whipped soy cream.

MAKES: 8–10 SLICES

²/₃ cup/1¹/₂ sticks unsalted butter
³/₄ cup superfine sugar
Scant 1 cup ground almonds
³/₄ cup instant polenta
4 eggs, beaten
Finely grated zest and juice of 1 large lemon
1 teaspoon gluten-free baking powder
¹/₂ cup raspberries
¹/₂ cup blueberries
Urefined superfine sugar, for sprinkling

NUTRITIONAL NOTE
This cake is suitable for gluten-free and wheat-free diets.

1. Preheat the oven to 350°F. Grease and line the bottom of a 8-inch round cake pan.

2. Beat the butter and sugar together in a bowl until creamy. Add the ground almonds, polenta, eggs, lemon zest and juice, and baking powder and mix well. Add the raspberries and blueberries and stir in gently to mix.

3. Spoon the mixture into the prepared pan and smooth the surface. Bake in the oven for about 40 minutes, or until lightly browned and firm to the touch.

4. Remove the cake from the oven and leave to cool slightly in the pan, then turn out and place on a serving plate. Sprinkle with unrefined superfine sugar and serve slightly warm or cold.

RICH FRUIT Cake

This cake is suitable for those allergic to eggs, wheat, or dairy. It will keep for up to 1 week in a cool place or in the refrigerator.

MAKES: 8–10 SLICES

1 cup golden raisins

$^2/_3$ cup dried apricots, chopped

$^2/_3$ cup raisins

$^1/_3$ cup dried prunes, chopped

12 ounces cold mashed pumpkin flesh

2 teaspoons finely grated lemon zest

4 tablespoons sunflower oil

1 cup soy flour

$1^2/_3$ cups rice flour

1 tablespoon gluten-free baking powder

1 teaspoon ground cinnamon

2 teaspoons ground pumpkin pie spice

1. Put the golden raisins, apricots, raisins, and prunes into a saucepan with 2 cups of water. Bring to a boil, then remove the pan from the heat and stir in the pumpkin, lemon zest, and sunflower oil. Cover and leave until completely cold.

2. Preheat the oven to 325°F. Grease and line a deep 8-inch round cake pan. Sift the flours, baking powder, and ground spices into a bowl, then stir this into the fruit mixture, mixing well. Spoon the mixture into the prepared pan and smooth the surface.

3. Bake in the oven for about $1^1/_4$–$1^1/_2$ hours, or until firm to the touch. Remove the cake from the oven, cover with foil, and leave in the tin until completely cold, then turn out and serve in slices.

NUTRITIONAL NOTE
This cake is suitable for wheat-free, dairy-free, sugar-free, egg-free, and nut-free diets.

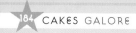

LIME & COCONUT Cake

Make this cake in the summer, fill the center with fresh fruit and serve with iced tea.

MAKES: 16 SLICES

1 cup dairy-free margarine
1 cup unrefined sugar
Finely grated zest of 2 limes
4 eggs, separated
2/3 cup gluten-free all-purpose flour
2/3 cup rice flour
2 teaspoons gluten-free baking
  powder
1/2 cup sweetened and tenderized
  shredded coconut
8 1/2 fluid ounces goat's or sheep's
  milk natural yogurt

FOR THE ICING & DECORATION
2 1/4 cups powdered sugar, sifted
Finely grated zest of 1 lime
About 2 tablespoons freshly squeezed
  lime juice
Toasted flakes of fresh coconut and
  fine strips of lime peel (optional)

1. Preheat the oven to 350°F. Grease a 1 1/2-quart round-bottomed ring pan.

2. Put the margarine, sugar, lime zest, and egg yolks in a bowl and beat together until well mixed. Sift the flours and baking powder over the egg yolk mixture and fold in together with the coconut and yogurt. Mix well.

3. Whisk the egg whites in a separate bowl until soft peaks form. Fold one-third of the whisked egg whites into the cake mixture to loosen it, then fold in the remainder. Spoon the mixture into the prepared pan and smooth the surface.

4. Bake in the oven for about 30 minutes, or until golden brown and firm to the touch. Cool in the pan for about 10 minutes, then turn out onto a wire rack and leave to cool completely.

5. To make the icing, put the powdered sugar in a bowl. Add the grated lime zest, then stir in enough lime juice to make a thick pouring consistency. Pour the icing over the cold cake and decorate with toasted coconut flakes and strips of lime peel, if you like. Serve in slices.

NUTRITIONAL NOTE
This cake is suitable for gluten-free and dairy-free diets.

INDEX

D

##

F

RECIPE CREDITS

VALERIE BARRETT: Pages 24, 28, 31, 32, 39, 44, 49, 64, 68, 72, 75, 80, 84, 90, 92, 94, 96, 102, 104, 105, 111, 116, 118, 119, 120, 125, 126, 170, 172, 173, 174, 175, 176, 178, 179, 180, 182, 183, 184.

CAROLINE BARTY: Pages 46, 55, 93.

JENNI FLEETWOOD: Page 79.

MAGGIE MAYHEW: Pages 25, 27, 48, 56, 58, 59, 60, 62, 63, 66, 78, 83, 87, 101, 132, 133, 134, 136, 137, 139, 144, 147, 151, 154, 157, 158, 166, 167.

CAROL TENNANT: Pages 42, 43, 82, 100.

PHILIPPA VANSTONE: Pages 22, 26, 30, 34, 35, 36, 38, 40, 50, 54, 65, 69, 70, 71, 76, 86, 98, 99, 108, 110, 112, 114, 115, 122, 124, 128, 140, 142, 143, 146, 150, 153, 160, 161, 162, 163, 164.

LIZ WOLF-COHEN: Pages 74, 138, 152.

SUSAN WOLK: Pages 148, 156.